D0118889

The
Hindenburg

The Hindenburg

Gina De Angelis

CHELSEA HOUSE PUBLISHERS
Philadelphia

Frontis: Nearly three football fields long, the luxury airship *Hindenburg* carried passengers in comfort across the Atlantic Ocean during the 1930s.

Cover photos: Corbis/Bettmann-UPI

CHELSEA HOUSE PUBLISHERS

Editor in Chief Stephen Reginald
Production Manager Pamela Loos
Art Director Sara Davis
Director of Photography Judy L. Hasday
Managing Editor James D. Gallagher
Senior Production Editor J. Christopher Higgins

Staff for THE *HINDENBURG*

Senior Editor LeeAnne Gelletly
Associate Art Director/Designer Takeshi Takahashi
Picture Researcher Patricia Burns
Cover Designer Takeshi Takahashi

3 5 7 9 8 6 4 2

The Chelsea House World Wide Web address is
http://www.chelseahouse.com

Library of Congress Cataloging-in-Publication Data

De Angelis, Gina.
The Hindenburg / Gina De Angelis.
  p. cm. — (Great disasters)
Includes bibliographical references and index.
Summary: Describes the development and early flights of airships and the disastrous explosion of the passenger airship Hindenburg at a New Jersey airfield on May 6, 1937, in which thirty-six people were killed.

ISBN 0-7910-5272-9

1. Hindenburg (Airship)—Juvenile literature. 2. Aircraft accidents—New Jersey—Juvenile literature. 3. Airships—History—Juvenile literature. [1. Hindenburg (Airship) 2. Airships. 3. Aircraft accidents.] I. Title. II. Great disasters and their reforms.

TL659.H5 D44 2000
363.12'465—dc21
                                      00-027360

Contents

GREAT DISASTERS
REFORMS and RAMIFICATIONS

Jill McCaffrey
National Chairman
Armed Forces Emergency Services
American Red Cross

Introduction

D isasters have always been a source of fascination and awe. Tales of a great flood that nearly wipes out all life are among humanity's oldest recorded stories, dating at least from the second millennium B.C., and they appear in cultures from the Middle East to the Arctic Circle to the southernmost tip of South America and the islands of Polynesia. Typically gods are at the center of these ancient disaster tales—which is perhaps not too surprising, given the fact that the tales originated during a time when human beings were at the mercy of natural forces they did not understand.

To a great extent, we still are at the mercy of nature, as anyone who reads the newspapers or watches nightly news broadcasts can attest.

Hurricanes, earthquakes, tornados, wildfires, and floods continue to exact a heavy toll in suffering and death, despite our considerable knowledge of the workings of the physical world. If science has offered only limited protection from the consequences of natural disasters, it has in no way diminished our fascination with them. Perhaps that's because the scale and power of natural disasters force us as individuals to confront our relatively insignificant place in the physical world and remind us of the fragility and transience of our lives. Perhaps it's because we can imagine ourselves in the midst of dire circumstances and wonder how we would respond. Perhaps it's because disasters seem to bring out the best and worst instincts of humanity: altruism and selfishness, courage and cowardice, generosity and greed.

As one of the national chairmen of the American Red Cross, a humanitarian organization that provides relief for victims of disasters, I have had the privilege of seeing some of humanity's best instincts. I have witnessed communities pulling together in the face of trauma; I have seen thousands of people answer the call to help total strangers in their time of need.

Of course, helping victims after a tragedy is not the only way, or even the best way, to deal with disaster. In many cases planning and preparation can minimize damage and loss of life—or even avoid a disaster entirely. For, as history repeatedly shows, many disasters are caused not by nature but by human folly, shortsightedness, and unethical conduct. For example, when a land developer wanted to create a lake for his exclusive resort club in Pennsylvania's Allegheny Mountains in 1880, he ignored expert warnings and cut corners in reconstructing an earthen dam. On May 31, 1889, the dam gave way, unleashing 20 million tons of water on the towns below. The Johnstown Flood, the deadliest in American history, claimed more than 2,200 lives. Greed and negligence would figure prominently in the Triangle Shirtwaist Company fire in 1911. Deplorable conditions in the garment sweatshop, along with a failure to give any thought to the safety of workers, led to the tragic deaths of 146 persons. Technology outstripped wisdom only a year later, when the designers of the luxury liner *Titanic* smugly declared their state-of-the-art ship "unsinkable," seeing no need to provide lifeboat capacity for everyone onboard. On the night of April 14, 1912, more than 1,500 passengers and crew paid for this hubris with their lives after the ship collided with an iceberg and sank. But human catastrophes aren't always the unforeseen consequences of carelessness or folly. In the 1940s the leaders of Nazi Germany purposefully and systematically set out to exterminate all Jews, along with Gypsies, homosexuals, the mentally ill, and other so-called undesirables. More recently terrorists have targeted random members of society, blowing up airplanes and buildings in an effort to advance their political agendas.

The books in the GREAT DISASTERS: REFORMS AND RAMIFICA-TIONS series examine these and other famous disasters, natural and human made. They explain the causes of the disasters, describe in detail how events unfolded, and paint vivid portraits of the people caught up in dangerous circumstances. But these books are more than just accounts of what happened to whom and why. For they place the disasters in historical perspective, showing how people's attitudes and actions changed and detailing the steps society took in the wake of each calamity. And in the end, the most important lesson we can learn from any disaster—as well as the most fitting tribute to those who suffered and died—is how to avoid a repeat in the future.

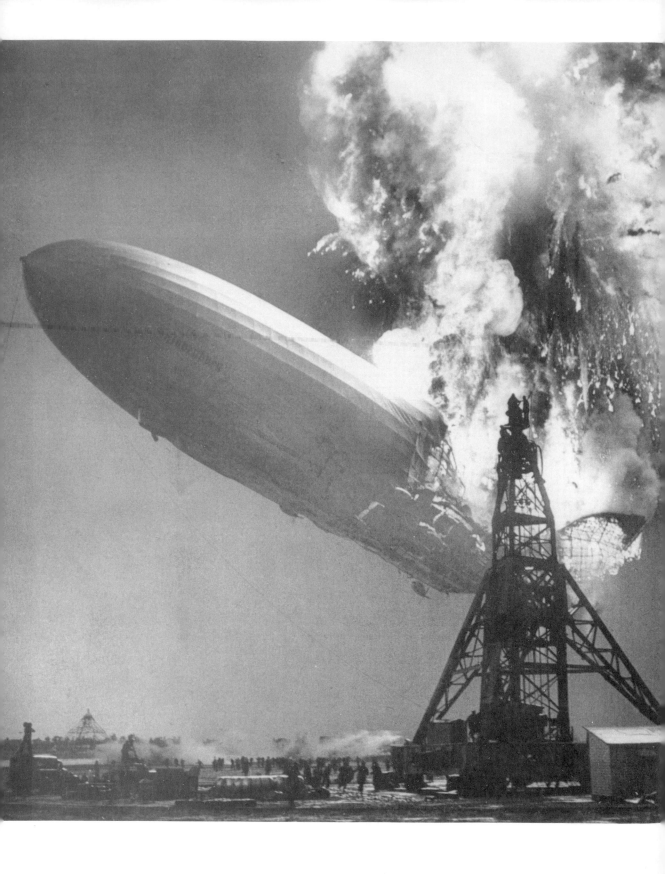

The nose mooring lines had already been dropped to the 248-member landing crew when the German luxury airship *Hindenburg* suddenly burst into flames.

Fire in the Sky

The evening of May 6, 1937, was overcast at Lakehurst Naval Air Station in New Jersey. The crowd looked expectantly for the 800-foot silver airship's arrival. It was several hours late because the commander, Captain Max Pruss, wanted to avoid a thunderstorm in the Lakehurst area. The families and friends of passengers had been waiting for a long time, some since morning. Finally the huge, cigar-shaped ship appeared in the sky a few minutes after 7 P.M.

The children and sightseers in the crowd were no doubt excited; so, too, were the civilian ground crew volunteers, who would be paid a dollar each for helping out. The *Hindenburg* was the newest and perhaps the most famous airship ever built. Unlike other airships, particularly those built for military use, the *Hindenburg* carried its passengers in comfortable surroundings much like the great ocean liners of the day. But unlike those vessels, the *Hindenburg* could cross the Atlantic in only two and a half days, rather than in a week or more. And unlike the Zeppelin company's other ship, the *Graf Zeppelin*, which carried passengers from Europe to Brazil for a few thousand dollars, the *Hindenburg* carried passengers for about $400 each.

About twice as long as today's biggest jumbo jets and nearly 100 feet longer than the biggest battleship of the era, the *Hindenburg* was a luxurious way to travel. Each passenger's berth featured hot and cold running water. The airship had its own bar, a huge dining room with real china and flatware and excellent world-class food and wine, and promenade decks where the passengers could look out of huge windows at the ground passing below. There was even a smoking room and a lounge with a grand piano in it. And unlike today's jet planes, the *Hindenburg* was quiet—passengers could sometimes hear the shouts of people below and the cry of birds in the air. With the windows open, there was no draft in or out when the ship was under way.

Many famous and even royal people traveled repeatedly on the *Hindenburg*; it was a glamorous way to go. To many spectators at Lakehurst, just seeing the great new ship moor to its mast at the station would be exciting, to say the least. For most of the ground crew, reporters, and newsreel cameramen, though, it was a routine flight. The *Hindenburg* had begun transatlantic passenger service the previous year and had made several safe landings at Lakehurst. No one expected this landing to be any different.

The ship was able to float despite the weight of its own frame, cover, engines, fuel, cargo, crew, passengers, and baggage because it was filled with more than 7 million cubic feet of hydrogen, a gas that is much lighter

than air. The hydrogen was contained inside more than a dozen huge bags, called cells, located inside the rigid frame of the ship. It also carried several tons of water ballast—extra weight that could be dropped when necessary—and each gas cell had valves that could allow some of the hydrogen to escape when the ship needed to descend. Although the *Hindenburg* had been designed to use helium, another lighter-than-air gas, it was filled with hydrogen instead.

Hydrogen, unlike helium, is flammable. When mixed with even a tiny amount of ordinary air, it becomes explosive. The German makers of the airship were well aware of this but believed that the ship was perfectly safe because they had taken precautions to prevent sparks or fire. For example, the crew members wore asbestos suits

Accommodations on the *Hindenburg* included a dining area and promenade decks, where passengers could look out through slanted observation windows— some of which opened to let in fresh ocean breezes.

and felt boots whenever they went inside the great ship's interior, near its gasbags. This way, no static electricity could build up. Crew member's suits had no buttons or zippers, or indeed anything that might cause a spark. All the walkways and ladders in the upper part of the ship were coated with rubber.

Passengers were made aware of the possible risks as well: all matches and cigarette lighters were confiscated when passengers stepped aboard. (These materials would be returned at landing.) The only cigarette lighter on board was chained to the wall in the smoking room, which was pressurized to prevent any stray hydrogen from leaking in. People had to pass through a special air lock to even get to the smoking room. And when passengers left the room, they were examined by a crew member to ensure that they carried no lit cigarettes, cigars, or pipes, and that they had no ashes or sparks on their clothing.

Even the four 1,300-horsepower Daimler-Benz diesel engines that drove the ship required no ignition (which creates an electrical spark). "They used a crude oil that wouldn't burn, it was claimed, even if a flaming match was tossed into the tank. Between these precautions and their self-confident enforcement of them, the Germans had absolute faith in the safety of the *Hindenburg*," explains John Toland, author of *The Great Dirigibles*. The *Hindenburg* had indeed been advertised as the safest airship ever built.

This particular crossing of the Atlantic, ending on May 6, 1937, was the first leg of the *Hindenburg*'s 11th round-trip journey to Lakehurst, and its 19th transoceanic trip overall. It had been comfortable, quiet, and uneventful, but the passengers were glad to be landing after the delay caused by the storm. At about 7:25 P.M., the mooring cables were dropped from the nose to the ground.

Then something awful happened: some crew members heard a sound like a gunshot. It was the sound of a gas cell igniting. Then there was a great concussion, felt hundreds of yards—even miles—away.

The stern (rear) of the ship was suddenly engulfed in flames. There was no time to think or to warn anyone—there was barely enough time to get away as the fire spread along the entire ship. It was a matter of seconds before each huge gas cell caught fire, one after another. Slowly the great ship fell to the ground, stern first, while passengers and crew alike rushed to the exits, windows, and hatches and jumped out. Then, slowly, the bow (front) of the ship tilted upward as the rear and middle of the ship crumpled to the ground. Flames shot 100 feet

In a matter of seconds, the airship was consumed by flames and completely destroyed. Miraculously, 62 of the 97 persons aboard survived the fireball.

into the air from the ship's nose, spreading to the entire front half, until the bow, too, finally sank to the ground.

It took only 32 seconds for the entire huge, luxurious ship to burn into nothing but twisted wreckage. In that time, miraculously, 62 of the 97 people on board managed to escape the flames and crashing metal. But 22 crew members, 13 passengers, and 1 member of the ground crew did not get away in time.

The crowd was astonished and horrified. Those watching the fiery inferno assumed that everyone on board had been killed. The fire was so huge and had erupted so suddenly that it seemed impossible anyone could have survived it. One man, Herbert Morrison, a reporter for the Chicago radio station WLS, had been recording his commentary of what he thought would be a routine landing. Instead his description became the first, and perhaps the most famous, on-site news account of a disaster of this magnitude. The recording is so harrowing, particularly when heard while viewing the newsreel footage of the disaster, that people today insist that they heard it live. (In fact, it was recorded and broadcast after the explosion.)

Morrison was so horrified that at one point he began to cry and could not continue speaking. One can hear in the tone of his voice—normal at first, and then changing to a sound of anguish—the extent of the shocking tragedy he was witnessing:

> Here it comes, ladies and gentlemen, and what a sight it is, a thrilling one, a marvelous sight. . . . The sun is striking the windows of the observation deck on the westward side and sparkling like glittering jewels on the background of black velvet. Passengers are looking out the windows waving. The ship is standing still now. The vast motors are just holding it, just enough to keep

from—It's broken into flames! It's flashing . . . flashing! It's flashing terrible! . . . oh, oh, oh! . . . It's burst into flames! . . . Oh my, this is terrible, oh my, get out of the way please! It is burning, bursting into flames and is falling. . . . Oh! This is one of the worst catastrophes in the world! . . . Oh! It's a terrible sight. . . . Oh! And the humanity and all the passengers! . . . I told you, it's a mass of smoking wreckage. Honest, I can hardly breathe. I'm going to step inside [the hangar] where I can't see it. . . . It's terrible. I— I— folks, I'm going to have to stop for a moment because I've lost my voice. This is the worst thing I've ever witnessed

On the recording of Morrison's commentary, one can hear the loud concussion of the ship exploding. Morrison's assistant, inside a nearby hangar, had to brush plaster dust shaken from the ceiling by the concussion off the recording machine.

For many years another passenger airship, the *Graf Zeppelin*, had safely crossed the Atlantic dozens of times, carrying passengers from Germany to Brazil. It had traveled more than a million miles without injury to a single passenger. The newer airship, the *Hindenburg*, had already made 10 round-trips in perfect safety—several times flying through rough weather without its passengers even being aware of turbulence. The *Hindenburg* was the safest airship ever built . . . wasn't it? What on earth had happened?

The Little Brazilian and the Crazy Count

2

Airships can be categorized into three different groups according to how they were built. These three kinds are nonrigid, semirigid, and rigid.

You have probably seen pictures or television footage of today's most well-known airship—the Goodyear blimp, which is often used to film sports events from high above the action. The Goodyear blimp is a nonrigid airship. It holds its shape solely because of the pressure of the lighter-than-air gas inside the airship's outer covering, or envelope. There are no solid parts on a nonrigid other than the gondola (for carrying instruments and passengers), engine, and tail fins—which attach to the envelope.

How did nonrigids come to be called blimps? According to airship expert R. D. Layman, the word dates back to 1915, when "Royal Naval Air

Service Lieutenant A. D. Cunningham playfully flicked a finger against the envelope of the SS.12 [a British semi-rigid airship] . . . and then mimicked aloud the sound that had been made." And so the word *blimp* was coined. (The word is onomatopoeic, meaning that it imitates a particular sound.)

The semirigid airship is similar to a blimp. However, the semirigid holds its shape partly because of gas pressure and partly because of the rigid keel that either attaches directly to the envelope or hangs just beneath it. The engines and gondola are attached to this keel.

In a rigid airship, such as the *Hindenburg*, a skeleton framework holds up the form of the ship. Gas is stored in several separate cells that do not need to be fully inflated for the vessel to keep its shape. Because the framework made rigid airships weigh so much, they had to be very large to accommodate the amount of gas needed to lift them.

All three types of airship—the rigid, semirigid, and nonrigid—have the same relative: the hot-air balloon. The history of lighter-than-air craft is longer than most people think. The first successful lighter-than-air craft flight took place in 1783 and is credited to the Montgolfier brothers, Joseph-Michel and Jacques-Étienne, of France. They created their first small balloon of paper and cloth. Because hot air rises, a small fire located underneath the balloon caused it to float. (A similar experimental balloon had also been demonstrated in 1709 by Bartholomeu Lourenço de Gusmão in Portugal.)

Joseph-Michel and Jacques-Étienne Montgolfier built several other craft, called aerostats. In the first public test, at Annonay, France, their 39-foot-long balloon rose to about 6,000 feet before landing nearly two miles away. The first living things to be carried in a Montgolfier balloon were a sheep, a rooster, and a duck. It was only after the animals landed unharmed that the king of France gave the Montgolfiers permission to put a person aboard their balloon gondola.

That same year, Jacques Alexandre César Charles was experimenting with hydrogen-filled balloons. The lighter-than-air gas had been discovered in 1766 by an Englishman, Henry Cavendish. Although the Montgolfiers knew about hydrogen, they had been unable to construct a balloon that could hold the gas. But Charles discovered that rubber-coated silk could hold hydrogen. He tested his first hydrogen balloon in 1783, only a few months after the Montgolfiers' first hot-air test flight.

The next step was to get to a specific destination by balloon. This was achieved in January 1785

The history of air travel began with the Montgolfier brothers' invention of the hot-air balloon. On September 19, 1783, the first balloon to carry passengers (a rooster, duck, and lamb) lifted off from Versailles, France.

by Jean Pierre François Blanchard, a Frenchman, and Dr. John Jeffries, an American, who crossed the English Channel from Dover, England, to Calais, France, in only two and a half hours. The age of air travel had begun.

In June 1785 another first was achieved. Jean-François Pilâtre de Rozier, who in 1783 had been the first person to ride a Montgolfier balloon, constructed a balloon in which to cross the English Channel. However, the combination hydrogen-filled, hot-air balloon exploded, and Rozier's death became the first known aerial fatality.

The fact remained that it was impossible to steer a

balloon. Blanchard and Jeffries had completed their trip only because the winds blew in the direction they wished to go. What if the winds were contrary? For many years, balloons were considered useful for observation, but not for direct travel. Still, they proved effective in the 1860s, during the U.S. Civil War, when both the Confederate and the Union forces surveyed enemy troop movements using balloons. These were always tethered to the ground, and no attempt was made to steer them.

During the mid-19th century in France, Henri Giffard found a possible solution for the biggest problem confronting aircraft of the day. He used the technology of the recently invented coal-burning steam engine to add power to a balloon, so that it could be flown wherever desired, regardless of wind direction. The French term for such a ship became *ballon dirigeable,* which literally means "steerable balloon." Later the noun *ballon* was dropped, and the word *dirigible* was adopted in English to mean *airship.* The Germans translated the English shorthand and called their craft *Luftschiff,* which comes from the German words for air (*Luft*) and ship (*Schiff*). Today, the word dirigible functions as a synonym for airship, although technically it just means "steerable."

Henri Giffard began experimenting with steerable craft designs in the 1840s and 1850s. He built one promising steam-powered dirigible that was 144 feet long and 39 feet in diameter. From the football-shaped gasbag hung the gondola, where the steam engine, propeller, and pilot were stationed. The three-horsepower engine and its fuel weighed several hundred pounds. Giffard was careful to mount the engine and exhaust pipe at the greatest distance possible from the hydrogen-filled gasbag, lest a spark cause a conflagration.

In September 1852 Giffard tested his machine successfully when he flew from Paris to Trappes, about 17

miles, in three hours. A later version of Giffard's machine included a cloth rudder, which Giffard used to steer the ship in a circle before awestruck spectators.

In 1855 Giffard built a bigger ship, which he hoped would be able to fly in less-than-perfect weather conditions. Unfortunately for the inventor, at the start of this machine's test flight gas began to leak from the bag. The ship tilted upward and gondola ropes broke, dumping Giffard and a friend to the ground. They were only slightly injured, but the ship was destroyed.

Giffard then went on a quest to introduce "air travel" to members of the public. At the 1867 Paris Exhibition he sold tickets to those who wanted to ride in his

By adding power to the hydrogen-filled balloon, Henri Giffard created a *ballon dirigeable,* or "steerable balloon." Giffard spent years presenting the new idea of air travel to the public. At the Paris Exposition of 1878 he provided rides using this giant tethered balloon.

Charles Renard and A. C. Krebs demonstrated the fastest airship of its time, the electric airship *La France,* at Chalais Neudon, France, in 1884. Their invention traveled at a speed of 14 miles per hour.

tethered craft. And in 1878 he carried as many as 35,000 people hundreds of feet into the sky. He did much to popularize the idea of powered flight. Still, Giffard never did improve upon his original steam-powered hydrogen airship.

But others did. In 1884, Charles Renard and A. C. Krebs built the first fully controllable airship. It was 165 feet long and carried a nine-horsepower electric motor. The ship, called *La France,* flew a five-mile course in only 23 minutes at the highest average speed then achieved by any aircraft: 14 miles per hour. Although the electric motor was definitely an improvement over the coal-burning steam engine, this new motor required batteries, which added a great deal of extra weight.

In 1885, Gottlieb Daimler invented yet another kind of engine—the gasoline-powered internal-combustion engine. This is the same kind of motor that would later be used to power the first automobiles. Using a two-horsepower Daimler engine, German inventor Dr. Karl Wölfert built and flew a dirigible in 1888. About nine years later, after considerable experimentation with this newer aircraft, Wölfert was killed when a flame from his engine ignited the hydrogen in the gasbag of his ship.

While Wölfert was working on his dirigibles in Germany, the Brazilian inventor Alberto Santos-Dumont was in France also pursuing the dream of controlled, powered airship flight. Santos-Dumont, who weighed about 100 pounds and stood barely 5 feet tall, completed and flew his first ship in 1898. Over the next several years Santos-Dumont crashed, rebuilt, tested, and often crashed again several airships of his own design. The fashionable, daring little Brazilian was the hit of Paris, and his dirigibles were the talk of France.

Within the next decade, however, Santos-Dumont would move from experimenting with lighter-than-air craft to developing the heavier-than-air flying machines. In fact, in the early years of the 20th century, many people believed that Alberto Santos-Dumont invented the first airplane. However, his first heavier-than-air machine, which flew before a cheering Paris crowd in 1906, could fly only in a straight line. Orville and Wilbur Wright, by contrast, had flown their first heavier-than-air craft on December 17, 1903, and by 1905, they had a steerable craft. But their tests were private, and the first reports of their successful heavier-than-air flight weren't universally accepted, explains Peter Jakab of the National Air and Space Museum in Washington, D.C.: "[Santos-Dumont's] was the first flight anyone had ever heard of, and so he got credited with the first flight."

But Santos-Dumont was not the only adventurer of the air. At about the same time that he was experimenting with lighter-than-air craft in France, a former German cavalry commander was pursuing his own dream in his country. Count Ferdinand von Zeppelin was designing and building his first airship.

Count von Zeppelin, known as "the crazy Count" because of his eccentricities, tested the first rigid airship, the *Luftschiff Zeppelin 1* (LZ-1) in July 1900. The 62-year-old inventor invited the public to view the ship's first flight, over Lake Constance. LZ-1 was an astounding 425 feet long. A small steamer towed it out onto the lake, and the dirigible, carrying five men (including the count) in two gondolas, was launched. For nearly 20 minutes, the airship flew about 1,300 feet above the lake. Then, unfortunately, a lever that helped steer the craft broke, ropes tangled, and the hull crumpled. As the ship set down gently on a sharp stake anchoring a buoy, it deflated.

Undeterred, the count fiddled with his machine and made two more test flights that year. Then he raised money to build the LZ-2, which flew in 1906. It made a rough, but safe landing; however, that night the ship was caught by strong winds and destroyed.

Count von Zeppelin persevered, raising even more money to build his next design—the LZ-3. It proved the most successful of his ships when in October 1906, on its first flight, it flew against winds of up to 25 miles per hour. Author John Toland describes the "Zeppelin fever" that overtook Germany after this feat:

> Overnight everyone, including Kaiser Wilhelm, wanted to be associated with the venture. The Count was decorated and honored by many societies. The Reichstag granted him financial aid for a fourth ship. "Zeppelin" cigarettes appeared on the market. The newspapers were filled with advertisements for "Zeppelin coats to be worn in the air." Pastry cooks made thousands of small "Zeppelins" out of sugar and marzipan; flowers were named after the inventor; and medallions containing his picture were sold by the thousands. And finally the government promised that

if the new ship, the LZ-4, could make a successful twenty-four-hour nonstop flight, a permanent yearly grant would be given the Count.

In July 1908 the LZ-4 was tested. It flew for 12 hours, making a loop over Switzerland to allow those outside Germany to have their first look at Zeppelin's new airship. Then the ship attempted a 24-hour nonstop flight, to win the grant the government had promised. Although the ship was forced at one point to land for emergency repairs, the LZ-4 completed the flight and landed safely near the village of Echterdingen.

Celebrations across Germany were already under way by the time the count's family and friends (including his young assistant, Hugo Eckener) were notified by telephone. The LZ-4 was tied down fast and left with a

On October 19, 1901, Brazilian aeronaut Alberto Santos-Dumont flew in his sixth airship invention from St. Cloud around the Eiffel Tower and back again, a distance of about seven miles. For this first-of-its-kind flight, he won the Deutsch Prize of $20,000.

crew of 65 soldiers to guard it. But suddenly the wind sprang up and caught the ship broadside, lifting it into the air. Those holding onto ropes were forced to let go; two men dropped from the rear gondola to the ground. A mechanic who was still aboard released the hydrogen gas, so that the ship would descend. It did, but then struck some trees and the remaining hydrogen exploded.

As early as the day after the ship's loss, people from all over Germany began donating money to help Count Zeppelin build another rigid airship. Although an old man by this time, Zeppelin was determined to continue fulfilling his dream of creating safe flying machines. He founded an airship building company, Luftschiffbau Zeppelin, and spent the remainder of 1908 building and testing new airships.

In 1909 Count Zeppelin, with business partner Hugo Eckener, founded DELAG (Deutsche Luftschiffahrt Aktien Gesellschaft), the first passenger airline company. Soon airship stations were being built all over Germany—Frankfurt, Berlin, Hamburg, and Dresden. According to Toland, the airships *Deutschland, Schwaben, Viktoria-Luise, Hansa,* and *Sachsen* "began establishing records of safety and performance that many people outside of Germany found hard to believe." In the next four years DELAG would make 1,600 flights in Europe, traveling 100,000 miles without injury to a single passenger. It seemed that the age of airships had finally arrived—and Germany was well in the lead.

Count von Zeppelin had some competition from others. In 1907 Walter Wellman, a journalist and something of a daredevil, built a 165-foot-long dirigible, the *America,* which he attempted to fly to the North Pole. He hadn't made any test flights, however, and he had to abort the trip after just a few dozen miles. In 1909 Wellman tried again—this time in a 228-foot ship with the same name. This ship fared no better than its predecessor: one of its two engines failed, and Wellman and his companions floated in the ship for two days before nearly crashing into the Atlantic Ocean. They were rescued by a passing steamship, the *Trent;* the *America* floated away into the sky and that was that.

In 1911 one of Wellman's companions, Calvin Vaniman, built his own ship, the *Akron* (not to be confused with the 1930s U.S. Navy airship of the same name). On its third test flight in July 1912, the *Akron* caught fire and exploded a few moments after its ascent near Atlantic City, New Jersey. All five men aboard were killed as a crowd that included the men's wives watched from the shore.

Meanwhile, in Germany, Zeppelin's passenger airline company, DELAG, was functioning successfully, and all the world was impressed. Indeed, Zeppelin's invention was to become so famous that to this day, many people think *Zeppelin* is a generic word for *airship*. (In fact, it's a brand name, much like *Kleenex* or *Band-Aid*. The word *Zeppelin* technically refers only to airships built by the Zeppelin company or a licensed user.) When World War I broke out in 1914, German officials and Zeppelin himself were confident that airships would prove a valuable weapon in the war.

The Zeppelins of World War I

3

In 1914, as World War I began to consume Europe, Germany continued building its famous Zeppelins. When the war began, Germany had only three passenger airships and six prototypes of military airships. By the war's end in 1918, the Luftschiffbau Zeppelin company had built 88 airships. A rival company, the Luftschiffbau Schütte-Lanz had also built several rigid airships, but these were used mostly by the Germany army. Schütte-Lanz airships had frames of laminated plywood; the German navy preferred the Zeppelin airships, which after 1914, were all constructed with frames of duralumin, an alloy of aluminum.

While Germany focused on building and improving its large rigid dirigibles, other nations, especially Britain, developed fighter planes and smaller, nonrigid airships—blimps. The British used blimps extensively during World War I, and ultimately had as many as 200 nonrigid airships for wartime operations—the number of British airships was actually greater than that of the German ones. However, British blimps were mostly used for defensive purposes: antisubmarine warfare, patrol operations, and reconnaissance missions (scouting enemy territory).

The German military used its rigid dirigibles in many ways. In at least one case, a Zeppelin was used to carry long-range payloads. And, like the British blimps, Zeppelins proved useful for scouting and reconnaissance missions. In 1916 a convoy of 10 Zeppelins was escorting a German fleet in the North Sea when men in the Zeppelins spotted a British fleet approaching the area. Because the convoy could warn the German fleet of the danger, it escaped before being attacked. However, during World War I, Germany was the only nation to use its airships offensively, in attack and long-range bombing missions.

A new invention, the spy car, made Zeppelins particularly useful for bombing missions during the early days of the war. The spy car was a large tub suspended from the airship. While the ship itself was hidden from view by clouds, the tiny spy car hung well below them. A man stationed in the car could contact the bridge, or navigational area, of the Zeppelin by telephone. From his position he could pinpoint exactly when and where the airship should drop its bombs.

At the start of World War I the British had few, if any, defenses against a Zeppelin attack, and London was a frequent target. British airplane pilots could chase after a bombing airship, but Zeppelins cruised at a very high altitude that planes could not reach. And although the airships were not faster than planes, Zeppelins at least attained a respectable speed. The German airships were also defended with machine guns, in the event that a pilot did catch up with them.

However, as the war progressed, newer, faster airplanes were developed. They carried a new weapon too: bullets laced with phosphorus, which burned with a flame hot enough to easily set an airship's hydrogen on fire.

Another newly developed defensive weapon—an incendiary rocket that could rise as high as two miles into the sky—soon made airships quite vulnerable. In response to this development, German airship engineers created "height climbers," a new breed of airship that could fly at tremendous altitudes and that was extremely lightweight. The undersides of these ships were painted black to better disguise them against a night sky.

Despite the airship bombardier's best efforts, though, hitting appropriate targets from a Zeppelin proved extremely difficult. The only serious damage that German Zeppelin raids inflicted in Britain was often to civilian property. Such damage had little strategic value—surely the German government would rather have destroyed military bases or munitions factories than people's homes and farms. Nevertheless, some historians believe that the raids did divert some resources toward defending Britain—resources that would otherwise have been used to support the war effort in France. The raids also had a strong effect on the morale of the British people, but perhaps not in the way the German command intended.

Even today, warfare waged against civilians is widely considered "playing dirty," and the international community is likely to respond to such an aggressor very negatively. Because of the Zeppelin raids, many people denounced German airship commanders and crews as "Huns and baby-killers." About 2,000 people were killed or injured in Britain by Zeppelin raids during World War I.

One of the greatest air raids of the war took place in October 1917, a few months after Count von Zeppelin's death. A fleet of 11 Zeppelins approached England at night, hidden from ground view by dark clouds. The English defenders were unable to spot the Zeppelins, while the airships were guided by lights on the ground and by smoking chimneys. The Zeppelins dropped their bombs and flew back toward Germany without being shot down.

Unfortunately for the airship crews, however, they soon encountered a storm with 60-mile-per-hour winds that blew them back across the English Channel—and right into antiaircraft fire. To avoid the gunfire, the ships rose as high as 20,000 feet. At that altitude the men endured terrible cold, suffered nosebleeds, and had difficulty breathing due to the reduced amount of oxygen. Somehow 6 of the 11 ships made it back to Germany before dawn. The other 5, however, drifted over France, into enemy territory. There, a fighter plane chased one ship, the L-55, to a height of over 25,000 feet. At such a great height, the crew became ill and blood spurted from their ears, noses, and mouths. To balance the ship, the L-55's captain jettisoned the water ballast, which was beginning to freeze into ice, and then brought the ship down.

Another of the four remaining Zeppelins, the L-44, was shot down by fighter planes. The L-45 landed safely and was scuttled by her crew. The L-49 also landed safely, but its crew members were so groggy from the high altitude that they were captured before they could destroy their ship. (The French copied the dimensions of the L-49 and years later it became the model for the U.S.-built airship *Shenandoah*.) The last ship, the L-50, smashed into the French Alps, knocking off the control car and one of the engine gondolas. The groggy survivors

who had been in these sections of the ship watched as the L-50 bounced off a mountaintop and drifted into the mist, carrying the remaining crew members away, never to be seen again.

Only a month or so after this disastrous air raid, one of the most interesting airship events of World War I occurred. The L-59 was ordered to fly to East Africa to resupply a German garrison that was desperately in need of medical help. Ernst Lehmann, who would later become a premier Zeppelin captain and Hugo Eckener's right-hand man—and who later still would be the last injured person to die as a result of the *Hindenburg* explosion—was in charge of supplies for the trip.

From Berlin, Germany, the L-59 flew to the airship station in Yamboli, Bulgaria. From there, the ship traveled on to Khartoum, Sudan, just 400 miles from its goal.

The Versailles Peace Treaty, signed on June 28, 1919, by Allied leaders (from left to right) Georges Clemenceau, premier of France, President Woodrow Wilson of the United States, Count Sonnino of Italy, and Lloyd George, premier of England. As part of the treaty's war reparations agreement, Germany had to give up all of its Zeppelins to the Allies.

But then the captain received a message by wireless to abort the trip—British forces were too close. Back to Bulgaria the L-59 flew, and although it had not achieved its mission goal, the crew was welcomed with cheers for their amazing feat, as described by historian John Toland: "The L-59 had flown for ninety-five continuous hours, at an average speed of forty-five miles an hour; 4225 miles had been covered without a stop, and there was fuel enough in the gasoline tanks for an additional 3750 miles." The ship had flown in temperatures ranging from about 20 degrees Fahrenheit to more than 100 degrees Fahrenheit. When the high temperatures had made the gas expand and escape through emergency valves, the crew countered the effect by dropping water ballast.

The L-59's mission, however, would probably have been successful had it not been aborted. Interestingly, the decision to abort was based on a fake message that the British had transmitted from Yalta, in southeastern Europe. Nevertheless, the ship's achievement was a remarkable one.

Then came the end of the war. On June 28, 1919, at Versailles, France, the peace treaty was signed between Germany and the Allied forces, which included Great Britain, France, Italy, and Japan. The treaty required that all of Germany's Zeppelins be given to the Allied nations as war reparations. The armistice also limited the size of Germany's armed forces, and forbade further development of large airships. (It would not be until the mid-1920s that the Locarno treaties would allow Germany to resume building large airships.)

Author Basil Collier tallies the number of German airships that existed:

> Of seventy rigid airships used by the navy, fifty-two were destroyed or forced down by enemy action, acci-

dentally destroyed or otherwise lost. A further six were
written off before the date of the armistice as obsolete or
surplus to requirements, so that only twelve remained
in commission when hostilities were suspended. The
army began the war with seven rigid airships and
commissioned another thirty-seven before deciding to
cut its losses. Of the total of forty-four, only two were
still extant at the date of the armistice, and these had
been laid up for many months.

Fourteen German airships remained, then, at the end
of the war. However, when news of the treaty's humil-
iating terms reached the German people, groups of

After World War I the
French claimed the
German-built L-72,
which had been built to
bomb New York.

disgruntled Germans, including former members of flight crews, broke into the airship sheds at Nordholz and Wittmundhaven and wrecked six airships, leaving only eight intact.

Of these remaining eight military airships, Britain claimed two, Belgium one, Japan one, and France and Italy two each. France and Italy also claimed one each of the two civilian airships—the *Bodensee* and the *Nordstern*—that the Zeppelin company had built for use after the war. Although the Allied nations were initially interested in pursuing airship programs, most of the surrendered Zeppelins were not destined for further missions. The airships soon deteriorated: "Post-war apathy and economic stringency resulted in the remainder becoming 'hangar queens,'" writes author Douglas Robinson. Japan's ship was broken up; Belgium's was dismantled and only parts were salvaged.

However, the United States was keenly interested in developing a military airship program. After the U.S Senate refused to ratify the Treaty of Versailles, a separate treaty between the United States and Germany was drawn up. According to the terms of the proposed treaty, the United States would accept a custom-built transatlantic airship as war reparations instead of requiring Germany to pay money. It was near the end of 1921 before both parties agreed to the treaty's terms and Zeppelin company director Hugo Eckener got the green light to start building the transoceanic airship. He had to obtain a special waiver in order to build the ship in Germany because its proposed size was much greater than that allowed by the Treaty of Versailles. The ship, known as the LZ-126, would have an interesting history.

Once the war was over and people had readjusted to peacetime pursuits, there was a new spirit in the air. People were mad for flying: airplanes, airships, anything. It was, for advocates of airships, an exciting time to be alive.

During the next two decades, the nations of Britain, France, Italy, and the United States would allocate vast amounts of money to airship research and development. Heads of governments in each of these countries were eager to develop airship programs, design and test their own inventions, and make use of the German airships they had received. Later Germany would be permitted to rejoin efforts to develop large airships, and all five nations would explore both the commercial and military potential of airship travel. It was the beginning of the golden age of airships.

The Golden Age of Airships

In the summer of 1919, the British built R.34 became the first airship to cross the Atlantic Ocean without stopping. The east-west crossing took 108 hours; the return trip only 74.

4

Before the war, Germany had been unrivaled in its construction of rigid airships. However, during the war, Britain had begun producing its own airships, although these were the nonrigid type. Britain actually used more airships for wartime operations than any other country, and by the war's end, had begun developing rigid dirigibles as well as blimps.

The British rigid airships of the time were nearly all copies of the German ship L-33, which had been captured in 1916. By the time the apportioned Zeppelins reached Britain in the summer of 1920, a British airship, the R-34, had already set several records. During the summer of 1919 the R-34 became the first airship to cross the Atlantic Ocean nonstop; the first aircraft of any kind to cross from east to west; and the first aircraft of any kind to cross the ocean both ways (from east to west took 108 hours; the return trip took only 74 hours). Earlier in the year the U.S. Navy seaplane NC-4 had been the first aircraft to cross the ocean, but it stopped in the Azores, off the coast of Portugal, before reaching Europe.

The early British rigid airships, however, did not last many years. R-31 was destroyed by accident in 1918; R-32 was destroyed purposely in a 1921 test to study its collapse; R-33 was used to experiment with hooking on airplanes while in flight, before being broken up in 1928; and R-34 crashed into a hillside in England in 1921. One British military airship, though, was of an entirely original design. Built from 1917 to 1920, the R-80 was used mostly for training airship men (notably American military airship crews) and for test flights. A well-built ship, the R-80 fell victim to the lack of skilled labor and the uncertainty of the future of airships, and was scrapped in 1925.

At the time of the signing of the Treaty of Versailles, the British government intended to build a series of dirigibles, numbered from R-35 through R-40. But after several airship misfortunes and because of opposition in the government, the expensive airship program was eventually abandoned. The R-38 was the last military airship built by the British, and it was intended for sale to the U.S. Navy (which would rename it ZR-2).

Begun in 1918, the R-38 was completed in 1921. It, too, was a copy of a wartime Zeppelin, although British designers had inserted an extra bay in the middle to give it more lift. This design change would prove to be disastrous. The German wartime Zeppelins were built differently from peacetime commercial airships. Zeppelins intended for military use were lighter, designed for more speed and maneuverability, and required more-rigorously trained flight crews than commercial airships did.

On its first test flight in June 1921, the R-38 was dif-

ficult to control and narrowly avoided an accident when its elevator controls (which tilted the ship either upward or downward) suddenly stopped working. Girders buckled, showing structural weakness, but the flight was completed safely and repairs were made. It was thought that sharp movements made to the airship's elevators or rudders had probably placed excessive stress on the structure, or that the rudders were overbalanced. Faulty design of the control panel may have been the cause of the problem with the R-38's elevator—a problem that, although it was repaired in this case, did not go away.

The Americans were eager to take "their" naval airship back to the United States. An expensive new airship

Throughout the 1920s both the British and Americans conducted hooking experiments— trying to have airplanes land on and take off from hooks on a dirigible. The system would not be put into practice until 1932, when the USS *Akron* became the first aerial aircraft carrier.

hangar at Lakehurst, New Jersey, had just been completed—it was the largest in the world. But the British commander refused to release the R-38 until it had been test-flown some more. Its fourth and last test flight began on August 23 and lasted 34 hours; the R-38 passed all the tests, and its commander and crew were pleased. As the ship was approaching the city of Hull, England, on the Humber River, onlookers on the ground noticed a wrinkle appear in the center of the ship.

The wrinkle turned into a crease, and the crease into a tear. Then there were explosions. The R-38 broke in two and looked as if it would crash into the center of the city. Fortunately for the city's inhabitants, although not for the crew, the ship fell into the river. Of the 49 men aboard, 44 died; only 1 of the 17 American crewmen survived.

"When the R-38 was lost," writes author Basil Collier, "the [British] government had already agreed that the Air Ministry's airship section should be disbanded as soon as this last ship was off their hands." And thus ended the British military airship program, in a wreck on the Humber River. Britain, however, would remain interested in developing commercial airships for several more years.

France, meanwhile, was just as eager as Britain to begin an airship program. The French government had received three Zeppelins from Germany as part of war reparations: one was a commercial airship, the *Nordstern,* which was renamed *Méditerranée*; the other two were the L-72 and the LZ-113. The French government hoped to set many new long-range cruising records with the L-72, renamed the *Dixmude*.

In 1923 the *Dixmude* made a successful five-day non-stop flight over the Sahara Desert of North Africa. Germany had built the ship to bomb New York City, and it had remarkable cruising range. But it had also been designed for very-high-altitude flights in good weather conditions; at lower altitudes, and in anything less than clear weather, the ship often ran into trouble. Nevertheless, the *Dixmude*'s successful flight had buoyed the French government's hopes, and it sent the *Dixmude* off for another long, grueling flight on December 18, 1923. Three days later the ship, and all aboard, disappeared.

The last message from the *Dixmude* was received on December 21. For a time the French government believed the ship had crashed in the desert, but a search turned up nothing. Then, believing the *Dixmude* had crashed into the Mediterranean Sea, the French conducted a search there. Finally, the body of the *Dixmude*'s commander was hauled from the Mediterranean by fishermen near the Italian island of Sicily. To this day it is unknown exactly what happened to the ship. Charred remains of the ship's cover eventually washed ashore, and a Sicilian reported having seen a very bright light in the sky off the coast on the night of December 23. Like many historical mysteries, the *Dixmude* has its share of devotees, reports John Toland:

> To this day some wishful romantics believe the control car and a small part of the structure dropped into the Mediterranean, but that the bulk of the *Dixmude* and her fifty passengers drifted into the heart of Africa. They argue that more wreckage would have been found if the whole ship had fallen into the sea; and they firmly believe that survivors of the *Dixmude,* or their descendants, will one day be found in the darkest part of the continent.

The French government had hoped to use the *Méditerranée* to provide regular passenger air service to Algeria. But after the *Dixmude* was lost with its captain, who had been a forceful advocate of airship travel, French officials realized they were not willing to invest so heavily in airships when such disasters could occur. The *Méditerranée* sat in a shed for a few years, and then it, along with the French navy's three nonrigid airships, was abandoned and dismantled. And thus the French government's airship program effectively ended.

Despite the disasters, the United States remained interested in airships, long after the interest of other governments had faltered. There were two main reasons: First, the United States possessed more helium than any other country. In 1903 Dr. H. P. Cady had discovered helium's existence in natural gas deposits, and in 1917, the U.S. Navy had discovered an inexpensive way to separate large quantities of helium from natural gas. Second, the United States had a greater need than the European countries did for efficient, long-range scouting vehicles, especially in view of the growing Japanese navy to its west. If military rigids that carried airplanes could be developed, the U.S. Navy could use as few as 10 airships, instead of 40 surface cruisers, to scout the same area of the Pacific Ocean. Airships carrying small airplanes could spread out and patrol a massive total area in a third of the time it would take ships to do so. The United States had actually begun conducting hook-on experiments between airships and airplanes even before the British had.

So in spite of the numerous airship accidents reported by other countries, during the postwar years the United States continued to believe in the promise of airships. Unlike its wartime allies, the United States continued to develop airships for military rather than commercial use.

A few months before the *Dixmude*'s disappearance, the first U.S.-built large rigid airship, the ZR-1, was christened USS *Shenandoah* (American Indian for "daughter of the stars"). The *Shenandoah* was nearly an exact copy of the German L-49 that had been captured by the French in 1917. However, because it was the first air-

ship designed to use helium (which is not as light as hydrogen), the *Shenandoah* had an added gas cell section. Another modification was an ingenious system that recovered condensation for use as water ballast. Construction of the ship began in Philadelphia in 1920 and was completed in 1923 at Lakehurst, New Jersey.

On January 16, 1924, a few weeks after the *Dixmude* had vanished, the *Shenandoah* was weathering a winter storm in Lakehurst. Suddenly the ship, with a skeleton crew of 21 aboard, was torn away from its mast. On board was Captain Anton Heinen, a German Zeppelin commander who was teaching the American crews how to fly airships. Although only an instructor and not in official command, Heinen used his expertise and leadership to save the ship from being immediately dashed into pine trees. Over the next day Heinen and the *Shenandoah* crew held their own, riding out the storm until the airship could return to Lakehurst. When it did, Professor C. P. Burgess, a Bureau of Aeronautics employee who had

The USS *Shenandoah* moors to the mast of the USS *Patoka*, the only Navy ship to serve as a mobile airship base. The *Shenandoah* was the first rigid airship designed to be moored to a floating mast.

been aboard during the incident, gushed, "Can you imagine a liner with two compartments caved in, a hole in her bow, half the steering gear torn away, bucking a gale of seventy-five miles an hour and returning to port? To me it was a rough ride but a good one!"

Another modification to the Zeppelin model allowed the *Shenandoah* to be moored to a floating mast mounted on a ship, the USS *Patoka*. All in all, it seemed the *Shenandoah* would surely prove to skeptics the safety of airships and their usefulness to the U.S. Navy.

The next year, in 1925, the *Shenandoah* flew across America in impressive time. Its first cross-country flight was remarkable, but far from easy for its crew. Crossing the Rocky Mountains in the dark and fog, and flying through treacherous passes and dust storms proved difficult work.

In 1923 Luftschiffbau Zeppelin had formed an alliance of sorts with the American-based Goodyear Tire and Rubber company. The terms of the Versailles peace treaty threatened the Zeppelin company's continued solvency, and the sheds at Friedrichshafen were to be destroyed. But the dream of continuing airship production was alive and well: Zeppelin licensed its patents to Goodyear, and the two companies formed the Goodyear-Zeppelin Corporation as a subsidiary of Goodyear. The new company hired many German airship engineers to work in the United States on Goodyear-Zeppelin ships. (Because the company had permission to use the trade name, its airships, too, are properly called Zeppelins.) The Goodyear-Zeppelin Corporation remained in business until, during World War II, its name was changed to Goodyear Aircraft.

Meanwhile, the LZ-126 airship that Germany had promised to build for the United States in the 1921 treaty was nearly finished; inflated with hydrogen, it was

delivered in 1924. Either because the U.S. Navy did not have enough helium for two airships, or because its budget did not allow for the purchase of more, the *Shenandoah* was deflated and its helium put into the new ship, which had been renamed the USS *Los Angeles*.

The airship was considered large by the Treaty of Versailles standards, which made Britain and France wary that the Zeppelin company had received special permission to build it. However, the *Los Angeles* was the smallest airship capable of crossing the Atlantic Ocean. Although designed for transatlantic passenger flight, the *Los Angeles* was not used for that purpose, partly because European countries did not have the helium needed to top off the gas cells. If the airship could not be filled with more helium for its return flight to the United States, it would not have enough lifting power to cross the Atlantic Ocean.

So instead of being used for transoceanic crossings, the *Los Angeles* functioned as an auxiliary to the navy,

A 1923 German-American business alliance resulted in the formation of the Goodyear-Zeppelin Corporation, a subsidiary of Goodyear Tire and Rubber. With the backing of American financiers, and later the removal of restrictions on building commercial airships, the Luftschiffbau Zeppelin Corporation could focus on building German luxury airships like the *Graf Zeppelin,* shown here in a 1929 photo.

In 1925 the USS *Shenandoah* broke apart in the skies above Ava, Ohio. Although 14 men died, 22 survivors in the aft-section "free-ballooned" to safety about 12 miles away.

where it was used for military maneuvers and scientific research flights. Although the *Shenandoah* had been the first ship to be moored to a floating mast, the *Los Angeles* did so much more often. The USS *Patoka* was the only ship equipped for such duties. While moored, though, the airship had to be "flown," engines running, so that its tail would not fall into the ocean. The *Los Angeles* was also the only airship to land aboard an aircraft carrier, the USS *Saratoga,* in 1928.

In 1925 the *Shenandoah* was refilled with helium, and the airship embarked upon a tour of the U.S. Midwest. All did not go smoothly. Over Ohio, the ship was caught in a squall line (the area between a warm, moist air mass and a cold, dry one). The warm and cold air masses twisted the ship in different directions. For several hours the crew struggled to control the *Shenandoah,* but it finally broke apart, with the bow and the stern coming down in separate pieces, several miles apart.

The eight men inside the control car died when it broke off and plummeted to the earth. Three more were killed when they were flung from the ship as it broke apart; another three perished when the engine cars were torn loose. But there was enough helium in the aft-portion of the ship that it ballooned to the ground, allowing the 22 men still inside to walk out safely. Of the 43 on board, 29 survived the harrowing, hours-long ordeal. The death toll would undoubtedly have been higher, perhaps even total, if hydrogen had been used in the ship.

Coming on the heels of the R-38 and the *Dixmude* disasters, the *Shenandoah* accident made many people wary of the wisdom of spending so much money on airships. Strangely, though, all three ships were of similar design: the *Dixmude* was an early wartime Zeppelin, the *Shenandoah* a copy of the same. And the R-38, too, had been built from a wartime design. But despite the disasters, the U.S. airship engineers continued to create and test airship designs.

In 1925, the same year as the *Shenandoah* disaster, the Locarno treaties removed all restrictions on the manufacture of civilian aircraft in Germany. The Zeppelin company was once again free to build huge airships destined for transatlantic passenger service.

The British dirigible
R 100 moors at Montreal,
Canada, after its first
overseas flight from
Cardington, England.

Great Expectations

5

During the First World War, Italy had developed a reputation for building reliable nonrigid airships. After the war the Italian government expanded into rigid airship development as well. The country had built a ship for Britain, called the SR-1, that made several successful flights before it was decommissioned in 1919. Italy sold another ship, the *Roma,* in 1921 to the United States. The following year, however, while undergoing stress tests, the *Roma* went out of control and crashed into wires, causing an explosion that killed 34 of the 45 people on board. Yet another Italian-built ship, the N-1, was sold to Norway and rechristened the *Norge.*

In 1926 the *Norge,* with a joint crew of Norwegians and Italians, became the first airship to cross the North Pole. This flight is all the more remarkable when one remembers that it took place a year before Charles Lindbergh made his historic nonstop solo flight across the Atlantic Ocean in his airplane, the *Spirit of St. Louis.*

The *Norge* was a 348-foot semirigid covered with three-ply fabric that was coated with rubber. The ship's three engines provided a respectable cruising speed of 50 miles per hour. On the polar journey, the 14-man crew, led by Italian general Umberto Nobile and Norwegian explorer Roald Amundsen, faced many challenges. Their ship was caught more than once in freezing fog banks, which caused ice to cover the control car windows, completely obstructing vision. Water that had worked its way into the pipes froze, and cut off fuel to an engine. Compasses stopped functioning properly, and replacement compasses also behaved strangely. But the *Norge* did reach the North Pole, at 1:30 A.M. on May 12, 1926. The crew members dropped three flags at the site to commemorate the event.

The explorers' goal was to travel on to Alaska, exploring uncharted territory. But it was a dangerous journey, especially when the crew was caught in yet another fog bank, with their compasses functioning erratically and ice encrusting the ship. Periodically, bits of the encrusted ice would break off, hit the *Norge*'s propellers, and shoot into the ship's fabric cover with a sound like a gunshot. A crew member would hurry to fix each hole as it was made. Fortunately none of the ice chunks punctured the ship's hydrogen gas cells.

After two days of nonstop flying, the airship explorers sighted Alaska, but the *Norge* was blown off course by a storm. Because of poor visibility, the crew members very nearly crashed the ship into the mountains. Another time, in an attempt to escape a fog bank, the *Norge* was raised to a higher altitude, where the sun warmed the

ship's hydrogen, causing it to expand rapidly and endanger the entire vessel. Faced with another serious storm, the captain and crew landed on May 14 at the small Eskimo village of Teller, Alaska—rather than continuing to Nome, their original destination. Unfortunately, even at the moment of their greatest triumph, the rivalry between Nobile and Amundsen erupted into a bitter public quarrel.

Two years later, Nobile captained another Italian ship, the *Italia*, on a second polar expedition. This time he hoped to explore the northernmost reaches of Russia, Greenland, and Canada, and to make a landing at the pole itself. Although the *Italia* was built to better withstand the problems encountered on the *Norge*'s trip, the crew on this journey was not so lucky.

In the first flight across the top of the world, the airship *Norge,* flown by Umberto Nobile and Roald Amundsen, traveled in May 1926 to the North Pole, and then beyond to uncharted areas between the Pole and Alaska. A subsequent expedition by Nobile would end in tragedy.

The trip began inauspiciously in very bad weather. On the way from Italy to Norway (the starting point was Norway's Spitsbergen archipelago), the ship's tail fin and propellers were damaged. After a four-day delay so the ship could be overhauled and repaired, the *Italia* finally took off on May 23, 1928, for the North Pole. The ship did reach the pole, early the next morning. For 7 of the 16 men aboard, this was their second visit.

Trouble developed a few days later, on May 28, when the *Italia* encountered bad weather. The ship had been struggling against strong winds for several hours when its elevator controls inexplicably jammed. The crew fixed the problem, but suddenly the airship began to rapidly lose altitude, and it crashed onto an ice floe. The control car was torn off and the envelope drifted away, with six men still aboard. Of the remaining 10, one died in the crash and two others were badly injured; Captain Nobile had a broken leg. Fortunately for the men, the emergency radio set had fallen onto the floe with them, and they could call for help.

Despite his feud with Nobile, when Amundsen heard that the *Italia* had crashed, he departed immediately on a rescue mission, along with many others. Nevertheless, it was 49 days before the last crash survivor was rescued (a 1971 Paramount film called *The Red Tent* tells this story). The rescue attempts themselves were dangerous, and several men risked their lives. Of the original 16 crewmen, 8 would survive. Nobile himself, despite his excellent leadership and solid encouragement of his men during this disaster, was disgraced by the crash. He eventually left Italy to work on airships in Russia. After the *Italia* disaster the Italian government ceased production of dirigibles.

Still, for all the failures and crashes that occurred in the 1920s, the belief that airships were an economical and tremendously useful technology remained strong, at least in the minds of many businessmen and government officials. Nobile's ill-fated second polar expedition took place the same year as the first successful airship passenger flight. In 1928 the LZ-127, better known as the *Graf Zeppelin,* carried 20 passengers and 40 crewmen from Germany to the United States. The dream of transatlantic passenger airship service had finally been realized.

A year later the *Graf Zeppelin* completed an impressive around-the-world tour in only 21 days. That same year, 1929, saw the first test flight of the R-101, one of two competing airships being developed in England and, it was hoped, the one that would make air service to India a reality. Although Great Britain had given up on military uses for airships, it was still interested in developing passenger service.

In 1924 the British government had contracted two different teams to produce a huge passenger airship for "service to the farthest reaches of the Empire." One contract went to the government team that had produced the R-38 for the United States, and the other contract went to Vickers, a private British company that also built airplanes. From the beginning there was great rivalry between the government team building the R-101 and the private company building the R-100.

The R-101's test flight in October 1929 revealed that the ship was too heavy. That would be fixed immediately, its designers said. To help increase lift, a new bay that would hold another gas cell was inserted in the middle of the ship. As German airship designers of the time could have told them, this was probably not a wise idea. The same design had been incorporated into the R-38 and the *Shenandoah,* although the latter ship had been better built.

The ship's competitor, the R-100, was tested in December 1929, and though it wasn't as beautiful to behold as the R-101, it could fly. The R-100 flew from England to Canada and back in July 1930. Although it suffered a mishap over the St. Lawrence River when the fabric covering the fins tore, crew members were able to repair the ship in midair. Based on its overall performance, the ship seemed more structurally sound than the R-101.

As a result of the success of the R-100, the R-101 was forced to make its first flight earlier than intended, in part to "show up" the Vickers ship. The British secretary of state for air, Lord Thomson, arranged to fly to India aboard the ship in early October 1930. To meet the deadline for Lord Thomson's much-publicized trip, the R-101's repairs were rushed—and there was no time to test the ship properly after the extensive repairs were made. The certificate of aeronautics, required of any craft flying in international airspace, was completed after a rushed inspection and handed to the captain just as the passengers filed aboard. Besides Lord Thomson, the ship also carried the British director of airship development; six officials of the Royal Airship Works, including the R-101's designer; and 42 crewmen.

Soon after takeoff the ship ran into a storm and developed engine trouble. Then the R-101's captain received a weather report that conditions over Paris were far from ideal. The forecast called for 40- to 50-mile-per-hour winds, and the ship had not ridden out the first storm very well. In fact, it had pitched and rolled much like an oceangoing ship might. Nevertheless, the R-101 continued on its course. At about 2 A.M., only eight hours after taking off from England, the R-101 went into a dive and bounced off the ground near Beauvais, France. Then it exploded. Of the 54 people aboard, only 6 survived. Among the dead was Lord Thomson.

The disaster horrified the British people: "In one

stroke . . . the elite of Great Britain's airship service had been wiped out," noted author John Toland. As a result of the R-101 disaster, no more rigid dirigibles, either government- or privately funded, would be built in England. And the better-built R-100 was never flown again, either. The ship, which had taken five years to build, was dismantled and sold for scrap. Now only Germany and the United States were continuing airship programs. And only Germany was developing airships designed for passenger service; the U.S. Navy was interested in airships only for military purposes.

In 1931 the U.S. Navy presented its newest airship, the ZRS-4, built by the Goodyear-Zeppelin Corporation and christened the USS *Akron*. Dubbed "Queen of the

Many British officials hoped that dirigibles like the R-101 could provide air service between England and India. In October 1930, Lord Thomson, the British secretary of state for air, and Colonel Richmond, the airship's designer, were photographed at the top of the R-101's mooring mast just before its fatal trip.

Skies" in press reports, the 785-foot vessel made its first flight in September of that year. Although the United States had experimented with hook-on airplanes as early as 1924, the *Akron* was the first airship to function as an aircraft carrier. The *Akron* and later the U.S. Navy airship *Macon* would be the only two such craft ever built to carry airplanes. The planes could be launched and retrieved while they were in flight. Indeed, once loaded aboard the airship, the planes had their landing gear removed and instead used "sky-hooks." The *Akron* would also set the record for the largest number of people carried by an airship: 207.

The *Akron* would set another, less happy record, too: its crash would be the worst airship disaster in history. In April 1933 the *Akron* was scheduled to make a trip from Lakehurst, New Jersey, up the New England coast. Although the weather was overcast, Admiral William Moffett, a great lover of airships and the chief of the Bureau of Aeronautics, had traveled from Washington, D.C., to go on the trip. Despite the foggy conditions, just before 7 P.M. the *Akron* ascended.

The ship carried 76 men, including several who had survived the *Shenandoah* crash eight years earlier. Still, the airship crew had flown through bad weather before, and no one expected anything but a routine flight. When an electrical storm appeared in the sky, the ship turned to avoid it and flew out over the Atlantic Ocean. Unfortunately, the vessel was soon caught in the center of the storm. Fierce winds forced the ship to rise and fall rapidly, and its girders buckled. Just after midnight the *Akron* crashed into the Atlantic Ocean. The *Phoebus,* a German oil tanker, was weathering the storm nearby. When its captain saw lights descend into the water, he turned his ship around, thinking an airplane had crashed in the heavy seas.

The *Phoebus* found only four men. One crewman, unconscious when rescued, never revived. Out of the 76 men, only 3 returned alive. Many rescue missions for the *Akron* had been launched when a British ship reported seeing men clinging to wreckage. One effort was attempted by the J-3, a navy blimp that had set out before the storm completely cleared; the J-3 also crashed. Luckily an amphibious plane was nearby, and its crew picked up several survivors. However, two of the J-3 crew died, bringing the total number of deaths caused by the *Akron* disaster to 75.

Hovering over the boroughs of New York City on November 2, 1931, the navy dirigible USS *Akron* (front) and the USS *Los Angeles* (upper right) head south for Lakehurst Naval Air Station in New Jersey.

USS *Falcon* crew haul the wreckage of the *Akron* out of the Atlantic Ocean. The 1933 crash resulted in the deaths of 75 men.

The navy possessed another Zeppelin-built airship, the USS *Macon*, which was christened in 1933, after the *Akron* crash. On this ship, after all the disasters, hung the hopes of the U.S. government and the navy. The *Macon* functioned successfully as a navy auxiliary, performing well during maneuvers in the Caribbean and in the Pacific in 1934. "That year the *Macon* won many friends in Congress," Toland writes. "As 1934 ended it seemed that the dirigible was at last coming of age in America."

In February 1935 the *Macon* embarked on more fleet maneuvers off the coast of California. On the way back to its base at Sunnyvale, the ship ran into a storm. Just after 5 P.M. a gust of wind rocked the *Macon*. As the captain turned the ship away from the storm, several gusts from different directions hit the ship, tearing away a section of the tail, which in turn tore open the rearmost gas cells. Although the ship was going down, the captain struggled to control it until the last possible moment. As a result of the *Akron* disaster, the *Macon* had been fitted with rafts and life jackets for each crew member, and the captain's actions bought the crew some time to prepare for the crash into the ocean.

Two of the 81 crew members aboard the *Macon* died in the crash. The presence of rafts and life jackets made a difference, indeed, in terms of lives lost and in stark contrast to the tragedy of the *Akron*. Nevertheless, after the crash of the *Macon,* the U.S. Navy built no more rigid dirigibles. The price, it had finally decided, was too high.

The *Hindenburg* contained 16 gas cells, such as the inflatable section shown here. The German dirigible was originally designed to carry nonflammable helium.

Building the *Hindenburg*

6

After the crash of the British-built R-101 in 1930, the director of the Zeppelin company, Dr. Hugo Eckener, was determined to switch from hydrogen to helium in future airships. Eckener hoped that because the United States was producing more helium, Congress might nullify the 1927 Helium Control Act, which declared all U.S.-produced helium to be government property, and prohibited its export. Or perhaps, Eckener hoped, the Zeppelin company could obtain helium from the United States by a special permit. After all, the new helium-filled airship he planned to build would benefit the United States, as the vessel would provide passenger service across the North Atlantic.

Eckener decided to scotch the construction plans for design LZ-128, which was for a ship of comparable size to the R-101 and R-100 airships.

65

Because helium had slightly less lifting power than hydrogen, the new ship that could lift the same weight would have to be bigger. The design used was LZ-129, later christened the *Hindenburg*. Construction of the new airship began in 1933 at the Zeppelin facility at Friedrichshafen, Germany.

The *Graf Zeppelin*, which had also been built at Friedrichshafen and completed in 1928, was as big a ship as could fit in the sheds at the time: 775 feet long and 100 feet in diameter. Even so, there was a clearance of only about two feet around the ship. But from 1929 to 1930 new, larger hangars had been built to accommodate a new airship. The *Hindenburg* was 804 feet long and 135 feet in diameter—bigger than the largest battleship afloat at the time. (For comparison, the luxury ocean liner *Titanic* was 879 feet long, longer than the *Hindenburg* by 25 yards.) The new airship would have much in common with the stately *Graf Zeppelin*, but at the same time, it used innovative design and construction techniques.

Each of *Hindenburg*'s four engine cars contained two diesel-powered engines, built by the Maybach Company, a subsidiary of Luftschiffbau Zeppelin. Each engine provided 1,300 horsepower for takeoff and 850 horsepower that allowed a maximum speed of 84 miles per hour. Each engine car, or nacelle, was mounted to the ship and connected to it by a gangway. A mechanic was stationed in an engine car at all times; there was room enough for one or two men and a work area. On the outside of each nacelle was a four-bladed, wooden propeller, 20 feet in diameter. The engines, which could run in reverse to provide reverse thrust for landings, did not require ignition to run: they were started by compressed air.

Another precaution against fire was incorporated in the design of *Hindenburg*'s engines. The *Graf Zeppelin* engines used a special fuel called Blau gas, developed by

Dr. Hermann Blau and produced by Union Carbide in the United States. This fuel gas weighed about as much as air. "The great advantage of carrying the Blau gas," according to Harold Dick, an engineer who worked for the Goodyear-Zeppelin Corporation, "was that its consumption by the engines did not lighten the ship, and hydrogen did not have to be valved off wastefully during the flight to keep the ship in . . . equilibrium, as would have been the case if gasoline had been burned." At times, however, when Blau gas was not affordable, the Germans made their own fuel gas by mixing hydrogen and propane, which of course was very flammable. In the *Hindenburg* the engines were diesel, and instead of Blau gas they burned a light oil, from the Dutch island of Aruba, that had a higher flash point than gasoline. The

Dr. Hugo Eckener (right), the director of the Zeppelin company, discusses airship passenger service with P. W. Litchfield, president of the Goodyear-Zeppelin Corporation. Eckener hoped a U.S. partnership could help his German company obtain the much safer helium gas for its dirigibles.

higher flash point meant there was less risk of fire.

The frames of Zeppelin airships were constructed of a durable, extralightweight alloy of aluminum, called duralumin. The metal had been invented in 1909, and later was manufactured in Düren, Germany. All German Zeppelins after 1914 were built using duralumin frames.

There were 15 of these huge, round duralumin frames in the *Hindenburg*. Each frame girder was triangular, adding to the strength and stability of the metal itself, and was reinforced at the keel. The frames were braced by 36 longitudinal girders. Hundreds of wire braces held the frames together and kept gas cells in their designated areas, even when the cells were overfilled. The wire braces also transmitted the lifting power of the gas cells to the keel, where most of the weight was concentrated.

Within this maze of frames and crisscrossing braces, several gangways allowed the crew to access various stations, such as the engine nacelles, the tail, the top of the ship, and the outer coverings of the gas cells. The tail of the ship consisted of fins (vertical pieces) and a tailplane (a horizontal piece); on the fins were two rudders, and the tailplane held the elevators. Just like a car driving in reverse, the ship would go left (port) when the rudder was turned to the right (starboard), and vice versa. Similarly, the elevators would make the ship descend when they were in an up position, and ascend when down. The rudders and elevators were connected to the control car by cables, but an airship needed to have its engines running at a good speed before these controls would take effect.

The ship's outer covering, or envelope, made of a tough cotton fabric, was not gasproof. The envelope was coated several times with "dope"—a mixture of cellulose acetate and acetone that was brushed on the outer shell. When it dried, the dope would contract, tightening the cover and making it waterproof. The fabric cover was secured to the ship's frame with doped lacing, which was then covered by sealing strips.

The fabric lining of each of *Hindenburg*'s 16 gas cells prevented leakage. The material used to make the gas cells in the earliest days of airships was rubberized cotton. Although the material could contain enough gas to allow a heavy airship to fly, the fabric was unsatisfactory because it allowed a great deal of leakage. Researchers developed a special gasproof material called goldbeaters' skin, which was first used in 1911. Goldbeaters' skin comes from the intestines of cattle. Although a very lightweight and excellently gastight material, it was also very expensive and difficult to obtain. For example, each airship gas cell required six layers of goldbeaters' skin. To obtain enough of this material to construct one gas cell, 50,000 animals were needed. Researchers developed an alternative design in 1914 by gluing three layers of goldbeaters' skin (instead of six) to cotton fabric. In 1918 silk was substituted for the cotton to make the gas cell even more lightweight.

Still, the Zeppelin company had trouble obtaining enough goldbeaters' skin for airship construction. Most of the material was imported from Argentina, which was under a blockade during World War I. Inferior-quality animal gut was sometimes substituted. During the war

The *Hindenburg* moors at Lakehurst Naval Air Station in New Jersey. The engines of the German airship burned a light oil that was less flammable than gasoline.

the gas cells of height climbers (high-altitude airships) were constructed with silk as a way to cut down on weight. Sometimes rubberized fabric was used, too, but that material created static electricity, and Germany simply could not obtain enough rubber.

One source says that construction of the *Shenandoah* required about 500,000 skins, and the *Graf Zeppelin*, 800,000. However, the *Akron*, *Macon*, and *Hindenburg* were constructed without using any goldbeaters' skin at all. In the American airships *Akron* and *Macon* (built in 1931 and 1933, respectively) a synthetic material made of gelatin and latex was used to seal the gas cells, effectively replacing goldbeaters' skin, and the *Hindenburg* used a similar gelatin solution. Later the *Graf Zeppelin*'s gas cells were converted and made with the new materials, too.

Six coats of the gelatin-and-latex solution were brushed onto the cotton fabric, yet the fabric remained lightweight. The gas cells were protected from the frame girders by wire mesh and by small-mesh ramie cord netting that had been waterproofed so as not to corrode the duralumin frames.

One problem that Zeppelin designers and engineers strove to solve was the question of ballast. To launch, airships would release water ballast from huge tanks inside the ship. But as water and fuel were used up during a flight, the ship would become lighter. Also, for every 1,000 feet that a ship ascended, the lifting gas, whether hydrogen or helium, would heat a few degrees, and when it heated, it expanded. To keep the gas cells from bursting, hydrogen gas, which was fairly inexpensive and easy to obtain, would be valved off. Then, more ballast could be dropped to keep the ship from descending too much if the gas cooled.

If the *Hindenburg* was to carry the more expensive helium, though, valving off the gas when the ship became

Workmen inside the Zeppelin LZ-129, also known as the *Hindenburg,* toil within the maze of metal girders, tanks, and mechanisms for controlling the huge ship.

too light was not an option. While the *Hindenburg* was being constructed, several alternative gas cell design ideas were pursued. The original design of the ship allowed for its 16 gas cells to be filled with helium, while 14 of them would also contain smaller internal cells that held hydrogen. These smaller cells, located near the top of the ship, could valve off the cheaper hydrogen from certain parts of the ship, or the whole ship, to keep equilibrium.

This design required construction of a second gangway that would allow crew members to monitor these valves. These internal cells were never installed, because it became clear during construction that the *Hindenburg*

After making its first transatlantic flight from Frankfurt, Germany, to Rio de Janeiro, Brazil, the *Hindenburg* enters the hangar at Santa Cruz airport. Note the Portuguese-language "no smoking" sign.

would not be inflated with helium—at least not for its first few flights. The second corridor, though, stayed. It could be reached via ladders from the keel up through three air ducts in the ship.

Other innovative ideas considered in the construction of the *Hindenburg* involved providing water for ballast. One concept was to develop a machine that used silica gel to absorb moisture from the air and condense it, thus providing ballast water. Much time and energy was spent developing a machine that would efficiently produce water, yet still be lightweight enough to carry on an airship. Also considered was a water-pickup system that would pump seawater into the ship as needed. Rain gutters, too, would enable the ship to catch rainwater for ballast; this method was tested on the *Graf Zeppelin* beginning in 1934 and was found satisfactory. Afterward "[i]t was common practice," noted author Harold Dick, "to 'brush' the edge of a rain shower with the side of the airship" to collect ballast quickly and easily.

And finally, the Zeppelin company considered installing a fifth engine that would burn excess hydrogen. Such an engine could do three useful things at once: reduce lift by burning hydrogen, add some power to the ship's engines, and also produce water for ballast. As it became apparent that the Zeppelin company could not obtain helium, most of these ideas were abandoned for the *Hindenburg*. In the end, the ship carried rain gutters, but the internal hydrogen cells, the silica gel extraction unit, the seawater pickup system, and the hydrogen-burning engine were not used.

Passenger accommodations aboard the *Hindenburg* were quite opulent even by today's standards of air travel, and much more luxurious than the facilities offered on the *Graf Zeppelin*. In the older airship the passenger cabins and lounge were located in the gondola, behind the control and radio rooms. But the *Hindenburg* had a smaller control car gondola, and its passenger accommodations were placed inside the hull of the ship. The two levels of passenger quarters were built in bay 12, which also held gas cell 12. (A gas cell was so large that even with the passenger quarters taking up room in bay 12, the cell there still contained 80 percent of the usual amount of hydrogen used in other gas cells.)

The upper level of the passenger accommodations, A-Deck, held 25 windowless sleeping cabins. These were very small rooms, and the walls and sliding doors were made of two thicknesses of outer-cover fabric with foam in between. The door of each cabin, even with its latch, weighed less than seven pounds. Inside each room were two berths (beds, much like those in the sleeper cars of trains), a tip-up washbasin with hot and cold running water, a collapsible writing table, and a signal for calling the steward.

A-Deck also had public rooms for passengers. The dining room was particularly lavish, with space for 50 people (or all of the ship's passengers) at once. Seated in comfortable chairs at linen-covered tables arrayed with vases of fresh flowers, diners would be served excellent food on china plates specially designed for the *Hindenburg*, and use real silverware.

The opposite side of A-Deck contained a writing room and a lounge. The latter room held a grand piano specially constructed with duralumin and covered with yellow pigskin so that it weighed less than 400 pounds. On either side of A-Deck were promenade, or walking, areas where passengers could enjoy the view through six large acrylic windows that angled outward at 45 degrees. Three of these windows could be opened. And at a cruising altitude of only about 800 feet, there was much to see.

The public rooms were decorated with artwork depicting the history of flight and the dining room walls showed scenes one would see from the *Graf Zeppelin* on its route to South America. The cabins and public rooms in *Hindenburg*, unlike those in *Graf Zeppelin*, were heated. The radiators used the water that cooled the engines to circulate heat for passenger areas.

On the lower floor, B-Deck, was a galley, or kitchen, containing electric appliances. A dumbwaiter (a small, pulley-operated elevator) carried cooked meals from the galley up to the A-Deck dining room. B-Deck also held a small bar and even a smoking room. Many precautions had been taken to keep the smoking room safe. It had only one entrance, which had an air lock. To prevent any stray hydrogen from entering, the smoking room was pressurized. Its walls and seats were also covered with yellow pigskin, a fire-resistant material. One side of the smoking room held windows that allowed a view looking straight down, and these were protected by a low railing.

The steward's room was on B-Deck as well. He conducted small tours of the ship for the passengers when requested (and when permitted by the ship's captain). Otherwise the passengers were restricted to the public rooms and their own cabins; the only access from the passenger quarters to the keel was through the steward's room. A separate dining area for officers and crew was also located on B-Deck, but crew accommodations were elsewhere on the ship.

B-Deck also housed one of the most impressive luxury features of any airship. *Hindenburg* was the first aircraft of any kind to offer a shower room "Passengers signed up to use the shower," writes Dick, "the first such luxury aboard any aerial conveyance. Designed to conserve water, it turned itself off after running for a certain predetermined length of time, perhaps leaving the passenger all soaped up. Waste water from the shower, along with that from the washbasins, was collected and saved as ballast in dirty-water tanks, as in the *Graf Zeppelin*."

Compared with air travel in the jet age, the great airships were truly a wonder.

The two-and-a-half day transatlantic crossing on the *Hindenburg* was one of ultimate comfort: a silky smooth ride, complete with marvelous food and impeccable service.

Not a Drop Spilled

Anyone who's ever flown on a jumbo jet or even a smaller plane can testify to how bumpy the ride can get when the airplane encounters turbulence. This was not the case on the *Hindenburg*. As historian David V. Wendell explains, "In the dining rooms of the *Graf Zeppelin* and the *Hindenburg*, passengers would take part in a contest to see who could stand a fountain pen on end the longest. The captains had ordered that the ship should never list at an angle greater than 5 degrees. At 10 degrees, wine could spill from a goblet. The Zeppelin company boasted that not a drop of wine had ever been spilled [on their airships]."

Have you ever felt the tilting of an airplane during takeoff and landing, or while the plane is banking (turning)? Another remarkable story told by Wendell reflects how even takeoffs and landings in the *Hindenburg* were smooth: "Weather delayed the liftoff of the *Hindenburg* in its debut flight in 1936, and at midnight a woman passenger approached the captain to inquire when they were to launch. 'Madam,' he said, 'we've been airborne for two hours.'" With such service, the Zeppelin company had reason to be proud of its passenger ships.

Variations in airship designs created differences, too, in how the vessels landed. The problem of securing an airship so that it could refuel, reballast, and disembark passengers and crew, yet not be destroyed by strong wind gusts while tethered to the ground, was an old one. Since the time when Count von Zeppelin sailed his earliest airships, many solutions had been proposed. An efficient, safe method of handling airships while on the ground was paramount if vessels were to be of commercial and military use. As experience showed what worked and what did not, airship landing techniques changed over the years.

Airships could be—and often were—easily damaged by clumsy ground crews or even by excessive wind. An airship was particularly vulnerable when it was first "walked" out of its shed; a sufficient crosswind striking the ship could seriously damage it. In March 1936 the brand-new *Hindenburg* was walked out of its shed for a three-day flight. A crosswind of 18 miles per hour lifted the ship and dashed its tail to the ground.

By about 1919 airship engineers had developed an effective mooring mast. The airship's nose was locked by cables into a cup located at the top of a high mast. The cup could revolve, so in the wind the ship would swing around, much like a weather vane. There was still some danger, however, that wind might pick up the ship and dash its tail to the ground. Also, when the ship was attached to such a mast, fluctuations of temperature that caused the gas to heat and expand would make the stern

After its fifth incident-free crossing to the United States, the *Hindenburg* is moored to the movable mast at Lakehurst Naval Air Station in New Jersey.

rise. Although these problems could be countered if the skeleton crew in charge of the ship was alert, German airship men in particular believed that this style of mast was too dangerous to use, even when crew members were monitoring the ship.

On one documented occasion, in 1927, the airship *Los Angeles*, which was attached to a high mast, was picked up by wind and stood directly on its nose. A sequence of photos of the *Los Angeles* doing a pirouette around its mast was published for the first time in 1973, in Douglas

Robinson's book *Giants in the Sky*. (Authorities understandably did not want such photos published while the ship was still in operation.)

A shorter, "stub" mast was developed by the Germans as an alternative to the high mast. The stub mast was not only lower than the original mooring mast, but it was also mobile—a great improvement over previous mooring methods. The ship could be attached to the stub mast while still in the shed and then hauled out via a system of docking rails to the mooring circle. This rail system required fewer members of the landing crew, and the ship could launch in light winds. The Germans used this docking rail system for both the *Graf Zeppelin* and the *Hindenburg*.

To keep the ship secured while it was not in flight or while in a shed, the tail was attached to a heavy railcar located on the rail tracks encircling the mooring mast. If the wind shifted or intensified, the stern could roll along the rails. This way the ship would simply turn like a weather vane, and there would not be excessive stress placed on its frame. By the time of the *Hindenburg*'s construction, both American and German airship men preferred the stub mast.

Landing techniques also underwent changes during this period. A system that used three wires for mooring was developed after one Zeppelin was forced into an emergency landing in 1917. But the wires took up a great deal of space and did not allow for refueling or repairs. Nor could the ship remain secured in this way for very long or in adverse weather conditions. For a time, airships had to be landed before they could be locked into the mast. During the 1920s, however, landing experiments produced the "flying moor" method, in which the ship could be moored before landing. First a mooring cable was dropped from the nose of the ship to the

ground, where the ground crew retrieved it and attached it to a wire running down from the top of the mast. Then two side wires were lowered from the ship and also attached. All three cables were reeled in simultaneously to prevent the ship from yawing (moving from side to side). (According to airship engineer Harold Dick, however, when Hugo Eckener commanded an airship, he actually preferred landing his ship first and walking it to the mast instead of using a flying moor.)

In the late 1920s and early 1930s there were high hopes all around for the success of passenger airships, despite the number of airship tragedies that had already occurred. Many believed that airplanes were unsuitable

A May 1936 aerial view of the *Hindenburg* (upper right) with the *Los Angeles* (foreground) moored to the mast at the Lakehurst Naval Air Station. The circle close to the hangar is the railtrack hauling up circle, used when the ship is "walked" out of its hanger. A track leads to the mooring out circle, from which the ship takes off or lands.

for long-distance passenger travel; they were small and could not carry much luggage, for one thing. For another, they had to stop frequently to refuel. They were also loud and uncomfortable. Airships, in contrast, were quiet and offered a smooth ride. They combined the luxury of ocean liners with some of the speed of airplanes, and they were cheaper to operate than either one. Airships, if they could be proved safe and reliable, were considered a better alternative for travel than passenger airplanes—which had, at any rate, not yet been fully developed. In fact, it would not be until several years after the *Hindenburg* disaster that transatlantic passenger airplane service would be offered.

The *Graf Zeppelin*'s successes during the late 1920s were especially encouraging to advocates of continued airship development. No other craft could match the *Graf Zeppelin*'s remarkable record of traveling more than 1 million miles without injury to a single passenger. The German dirigible gave exceptional promise of the safety of passenger airships when handled competently.

In one case the *Graf Zeppelin* was mishandled, with potentially serious results. On its first flight to America in 1928, the airship ran into a storm. An inexperienced elevator man (the crew member who controlled the ship's elevators on the tail) made a mistake and a gust of wind tore the fabric off the port tail fin. Although the ship lost control, the passengers remained unaware of the danger. Under the masterful leadership of Captain Hugo Eckener, the damage was repaired in midair—not without some danger to the men who fixed the tear, including Eckener's own son—and the flight continued to New York City. The *Graf Zeppelin* was welcomed with tumultuous uproar in various U.S. cities. And in 1929 it became the only airship ever to circumnavigate the world, a flight it completed in just 21 days.

The Empire State Building, built in 1931, was designed to serve as a dirigible station, although the idea proved impractical. This photo montage illustrates how an airship would connect with the building tower.

These high hopes for developing safe passenger airships were reflected in a special characteristic of the Empire State Building, completed in 1931. The top of the building boasted a mooring mast that was intended to service passenger airships. The mast was actually used at least once during a public relations event, but no large passenger airship ever moored there. The idea was eventually scrapped when a suitable system for disembarking could not be devised. Few passengers, airship designers realized, would be willing to climb down a ladder while more than 100 stories in the air. And, of course, only a few years later the *Hindenburg*'s tragic destruction would put an end to the talk of passenger airships. But in the 1920s and early 1930s the dream was still very much alive.

The *Hindenburg*'s first season of operation, in 1936, trumpeted to the world the possibilities of safe airship travel. The airship cruised at up to 84 miles per hour, an almost unheard-of pace. That speed reduced the time required to cross the Atlantic Ocean by several days; riding in the *Hindenburg*, people could now travel in opulent comfort between Europe and America in only two and a half days.

Throughout the airship's first season, as author John Toland writes, "the big dirigible had flown with unfailing regularity, in rain, fog, and storm, and had done much to allay the public distrust inspired by the terrible airship disasters of the early thirties. Not even the devastating hurricane that had uprooted so much of New England earlier that fall had stopped the *Hindenburg*. So calm was the trip that most of the passengers weren't aware they were passing over scenes of violent destruction."

To allay any remaining fears and to convince influential people of the great Zeppelin's safety firsthand, the *Hindenburg* made a special 10-hour round-trip flight over New England in the fall of 1936, dubbed by some as the "Millionaire's Flight." The airship carried 73 industry and government leaders who were, according to one historian, "collectively worth more than four times as much as all the wealthy passengers on the . . . *Titanic*." Combined with the safe record of German commercial airships over the previous few decades and that of the first season of the *Hindenburg* itself, this successful flight "sold" many Americans on the idea of airship travel. The Zeppelin company made elaborate plans to construct two more airships that would be even bigger than the *Hindenburg*.

In 1936 a one-way ticket on the *Hindenburg* between the United States and Europe cost about $400 (in today's money, about $4,320); the fare on the *Graf Zeppelin* was originally $2,250. By contrast, a similar journey in first-class on the most luxurious ship of the time, the Queen Mary, cost the passenger $280, and the trip took about a week. In 1999 a six-day voyage between the United States and Europe aboard the Queen Elizabeth II costs from $1,195 to $7,700. And a similar one-way ticket to fly on the Concorde jet, a journey that takes only a few hours, costs about $3,000.

The Great Depression, a time of great economic hardship for many Americans, was still in full swing in 1936 and 1937. Few people could afford the expensive means of travel that the *Hindenburg* offered, but many looked forward to a time when they could. A trip on the luxurious dirigible was not cheap, to be sure, but it was fast, smooth, extremely comfortable—and very prestigious. By the end of the airship's first flight season in 1936, everyone was convinced the *Hindenburg* would become even more famous in 1937.

The Aftermath and the Theories

The skeletal remains of a once proud airship, as seen the day after the fire.

Why did the *Hindenburg* end up using hydrogen instead of the much safer helium? In the 1930s, when the ship was being designed and built, the United States had the greatest supply of helium in the world. After World War I ended, the U.S. Navy had built a facility to produce helium near Amarillo, Texas. But in 1927, Congress had passed the Helium Control Act, which prohibited export of the gas. The U.S. government wanted to provide for its own naval airship program, while preventing possibly aggressive foreign powers from obtaining helium. At the time, helium was considered a potential weapon, so it had to be guarded and not shared.

By the 1930s the dangers of using hydrogen in airships was well known. The potential for disaster with hydrogen-filled airships had first been seen in the United States in July 1919, when one of the first Goodyear aircraft, the *Wingfoot Express*, caught fire in midair above Chicago, Illinois. The airship crashed through the skylight of a bank, killing three people aboard the ship and 10 people inside the bank. As a result of this tragedy and the 1922 explosion of the Italian-made airship *Roma* in Hampton Roads, Virginia, hydrogen was banned from use in U.S. airships.

During World War I, Zeppelins had proved to be useful weapons. In the 1930s the newly formed Nazi Party was very proud of Germany's Zeppelins and often exhibited the *Graf Zeppelin*, and later, the *Hindenburg*, as propaganda tools. These airships, the party believed, showed the world how advanced and technologically skilled Germany was. The Luftschiffbau Zeppelin company had already demonstrated that it had the technological expertise to build an airship (the *Dixmude*) capable of traveling from Europe to New York City. Now the U.S. government feared that Adolf Hitler, the German chancellor, might use Germany's new airships for military purposes, and he could do that so much more easily if he had dependable supplies of helium.

Hugo Eckener, the Zeppelin company's director, was anti-Nazi, and he hoped that by cooperating with an American Zeppelin company, his firm would receive special permission to buy helium from the United States, despite the prohibition. But this did not happen before the *Hindenburg* was ready to fly, and at any rate, the helium was very expensive, even for the German government. In the end, the company was forced to use hydrogen, which was much cheaper and more readily available.

The Germans were confident that if the hydrogen was stringently controlled, it would be safe to use. Its purity was tested daily. If the hydrogen in a cell had become debased by mixing with air, that cell would be

emptied and refilled with pure hydrogen. Other precautions were taken as well. Because hydrogen is an odorless gas, a garlic scent was added to make any gas leak easy to detect.

Harold Dick, who worked for the Goodyear-Zeppelin Corporation, was privileged to accompany the crews of the *Hindenburg* and the *Graf Zeppelin* as an official observer on many flights. In his book, *The Golden Age of the Great Passenger Airships: Graf Zeppelin and Hindenburg*, he relates a story about how infectious the confidence of German airship officials was. When other Americans, notably U.S. Navy men who had been invited aboard as observers, would express the view that hydrogen's use was perfectly safe in airships because the

Dr. Hugo Eckener (right) appeared before the U.S. House Military Committee in May 1937 to urge the United States to relax its laws against exporting helium. Many argue that the *Hindenburg* would never have burned if it had been inflated with helium rather than hydrogen.

Germans knew how to handle it, Dick had a way of changing their opinion.

> I would suggest to our naval observer holding these views that he and I should take a tour through the ship. We would climb one of the access ladders to the axial corridor which passed through a tunnel right in the center of the gas cells. When about halfway to the next access ladder, I would point out to him that there was about 65 feet of hydrogen on all sides of us and that if anything went wrong there would be no chance of getting out. The demonstration worked. None of those Navy men ever mentioned to me again the idea that hydrogen properly used was safe and should be used in any new or subsequent airships!

The *Hindenburg*'s destruction was not the worst airship disaster in history; many other airships had met with similar or greater disaster. And it is true that German airships safely weathered storms that American and British ships did not. But the *Hindenburg* disaster was the first time that paying passengers were injured or killed. It was also the first major disaster witnessed by photographers and the public. The photographs and newsreels, and especially Herbert Morrison's haunting commentary, were broadcast around the world. People were both mesmerized and horrified by the sights and sounds of the explosion. To this day, the *Hindenburg*'s fame is largely due to the films and recordings made of its fiery end.

The *Hindenburg* was the largest rigid dirigible ever flown; after it was destroyed, no other rigid airship ever carried paying passengers. The *Graf Zeppelin* was immediately taken out of service, in light of the tragedy and the public's utter loss of confidence in airship travel. After the *Hindenburg*'s very public end, and in the face of the sad fate that befell most of the other great airships, it became

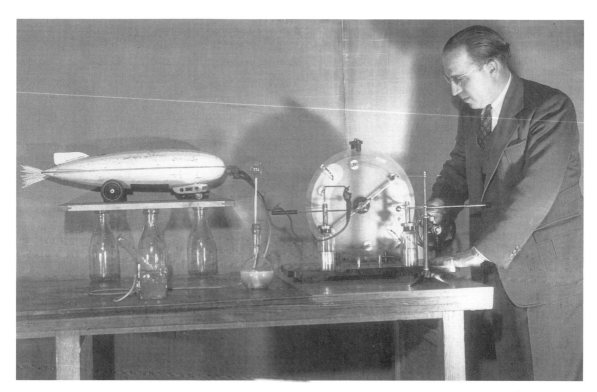

Michael Fiore used a static-inducing machine and a grounded model of the Zeppelin to support his claim that the *Hindenburg* fire was caused by static electricity that ignited escaping hydrogen. More recently some experts have argued that the flammable airship cover, and not a hydrogen leak, was to blame.

difficult to argue that even helium-filled airships were safe, particularly when flying through rough weather. And even if airships could be made safe, their expense no longer seemed justifiable in an age of rapidly advancing airplane technology. Nor did the cost of airship development seem feasible while an economic depression and global war taxed the economies of several world powers.

Even today no one knows for sure what caused the explosion that destroyed the *Hindenburg*. Of course, there were many theories at the time, including one that attributed the disaster to static electricity or a stray bolt of lightning from the thunderstorm that had passed through earlier in the day. Another theory blamed pilot error, engine failure, or both; still others claimed sabotage by an enemy of Germany or of the Nazi Party—or even an enemy of Zeppelin company director Hugo Eckener, who was disliked by the Nazi government.

For many years, however, most experts seemed to agree with the American and German investigating commissions assigned to determine the cause of the explosion. These investigators concluded that static electricity in the atmosphere caused an outburst of Saint Elmo's fire (a flaming phenomenon that is sometimes seen in stormy weather on airplanes, ships, or land), which then found a small hydrogen leak and ignited it. Author Douglas Robinson describes how one "noted authority on electrostatics and atmospheric electricity," Professor Dieckmann, testified before the commissions:

> [S]everal minutes after the *Hindenburg* dropped her landing ropes, there would be an equalization of the static charges in the ship and on the ground, and therefore the Zeppelin, having "become a piece of the ground elevated into the atmosphere," would discharge electricity into the atmosphere— the so-called brush discharge or St. Elmo's Fire . . . "such a discharge likely would have ignited any adequately rich stream of leaking hydrogen that reached it."

Although no one close to the mooring mast or on the ground crew saw such a flame, Professor Mark Heald, who was standing outside the gates at the Lakehurst Naval Air Station, described seeing a bluish flame on the top ridge of the airship just before the explosion. And since the ship had just valved off some hydrogen to descend to the mooring mast, it is possible that one of the valves may have stayed open, creating a rich stream of gas that a static electrical spark could ignite.

On the other hand, some who were aboard the *Hindenburg* insist that there was no hydrogen leak. An argument presented in 1997 holds that the type of explosion and the way the fire spread indicate only one possibility: that the dope, or varnish, on the fabric cover had

ignited, not the hydrogen. Retired NASA engineer Addison Bain, who has conducted much research on the *Hindenburg* disaster, believes that the ship would have exploded because of the presence of hydrogen, but that the fire did not start because of it. Author Jacquelyn Bokow describes Bain's research:

> Observations of the incident show evidence inconsistent with a hydrogen fire: (1) the *Hindenburg* did not explode, but burned very rapidly in omnidirectional patterns, (2) the 240-ton airship remained aloft and upright many seconds after the fire began, (3) falling pieces of fabric were aflame and not self-extinguishing, and (4) the very bright color of the flames was

Survivors of the *Hindenburg* tragedy, including the 13-year-old cabin boy, were photographed two days later. Many are wearing U.S. Marine summer clothing that was given to replace clothing burned off of them as they escaped the flames.

characteristic of a forest fire, not a hydrogen fire (hydrogen makes no visible flame).

Bain attributes the start of the fire to the *Hindenburg*'s fabric covering, not a hydrogen leak. The researcher points out that no one at the scene reported smelling garlic, which would have indicated a leak.

Bain—who published an article on his theory in the May 1997 issue of *Air and Space*, a Smithsonian Institution magazine—conducted experiments to test his hypothesis. He obtained from the Zeppelin company two 60-year-old fabric samples of a type used on the *Hindenburg*. Upon examination he determined that the material was cotton covered with cellulose nitrate and powdered aluminum. Unlike hydrogen, aluminum makes a very bright flame when burned (the U.S. space shuttle rocket boosters are an example of aluminum-based combustion). Bain subjected one fabric sample to flames and it burned instantly. He then subjected the second sample to high-voltage electrical fields in order to reproduce the atmospheric conditions existing when the *Hindenburg* made its last landing. The arc of electricity burned a hole in the fabric. However, when the sample was positioned like the airship had been—parallel to the arc—the fabric ignited and completely burned up within seconds.

Bain also found handwritten letters in the Zeppelin Archive in Friedrichshafen, Germany, that corroborate his view. In June 1937 an engineer had written that "the actual cause of the fire was the extreme easy flammability of the covering material brought about by discharges of an electrostatic nature."

Still others had another theory. Many people, including Max Pruss, the capable and experienced commander of the *Hindenburg* on its last flight, believed that the airship's destruction was caused by sabotage. Hugo Eckener had agreed with Pruss but was later forced by the Nazi government to declare publicly that no such thing happened; privately, at least at first, he was convinced that the *Hindenburg* had been destroyed deliberately. He told a reporter just that on the day he learned of the disaster.

Given the intense enmity between the Nazi regime and Eckener, such a theory is plausible. Despite Eckener's personal distaste for the Nazi Party, he had been forced to display the Nazi swastika on each of his airships. Hitler's propaganda minister, Joseph Goebbels, had demanded that an enormous Nazi flag be displayed on the hull in the middle of the ship, but Eckener had complied only with a smaller version of the flag placed on the left side of the *Graf Zeppelin*'s tail fins. And later, when the *Graf Zeppelin* flew over the World's Fair in Chicago in 1933, Eckener arranged for the ship to circle only in a clockwise direction so that spectators would see the right side of the fins, which had no swastikas. Unlike the *Graf Zeppelin*, however, the *Hindenburg* displayed swastikas on both sides, ensuring that the Nazi symbol would be visible to all.

During the 1930s, Eckener resisted as best he could as the Nazi Party appropriated many of Count von Zeppelin's great inventions. In March 1936, Goebbels insisted that both the *Graf Zeppelin* and the *Hindenburg* be used to encourage Germans to vote for Germany's annexation of the Rhineland, a demilitarized area established by the Treaty of Versailles in 1919. Eckener himself refused to be present for this event, even though it was the new *Hindenburg*'s first flight.

Afterwards, Eckener reproached *Hindenburg* captain Ernst Lehmann for having cooperated with the Nazis in the propaganda flight, especially because the tail of the ship was damaged when it was brought out of the hanger. Harold Dick, who was present at the time, describes

Swastikas adorn both sides of the tail fins of the new *Hindenburg* as it is "walked out" of the hanger on March 26, 1936, for a propaganda flight. Despite the objections of company director Hugo Eckener, Nazi propaganda minister Joseph Goebbels used the Zeppelin as a symbol of Nazi power—which some may have wanted to destroy.

what happened when the Zeppelin company director met Lehmann after the flight: "Dr. Eckener . . . angrily accused him in front of witnesses: 'How could you, Herr Lehmann, order the ship to be brought out in such wind conditions? You had the best excuse in the world to postpone this idiotic flight; instead you risked the ship merely to avoid annoying Herr Goebbels.'"

The Nazi regime dared not arrest Eckener, who had long been a popular hero in Germany as well as a skillful leader of Luftschiffbau Zeppelin. But when Goebbels learned of Eckener's remarks to Lehmann, he declared Eckener a "nonperson." Eckener's existence was officially denied; any photographs of him or mentions of his name were banned from all German newspapers and press releases. He was even threatened with exile. Under such circumstances, it is understandable that Eckener would believe the *Hindenburg* had been purposely destroyed by Nazi sabotage. In later years, according to one historian, the Zeppelin company director changed his mind and completely rejected the sabotage theory, even though it would have cleared his beloved Zeppelin of any fault.

The *Hindenburg*'s commander, Captain Pruss, believed that an incendiary device caused the fire that destroyed the airship. In 1957 he remarked that the control car instrument that monitored gas cell content would have told him if one of the gas cells was at less than 100 percent capacity. The instrument gave him no such indication just before the accident. In other words, Pruss did not believe there had been any leak producing a stream of hydrogen that ignited. He noted, too, that the fire had started between cells 4 and 5, where a ladder permitted human access. At least one *Hindenburg* crew member claimed to have seen a sudden glow in the number 4 gasbag just before the fire.

Even if a saboteur had wanted to destroy the *Hindenburg* because it was a symbol of Nazi power, he may not have wanted to kill passengers in the process. In 1938, Charles Rosendahl, an experienced airship man who in 1937 had been commander of Lakehurst Naval Air Station, published his theory that an incendiary device may have been placed in the *Hindenburg*. According to Rosendahl, the device might have been set it go off after 6:00 P.M., which was when the ship was supposed to be moored to the mast and empty of passengers and most of the crew. Captain Pruss claimed in later years that he knew which passenger may have committed such an act— a man whom Pruss considered suspicious at the time.

Other sources also note that one of the crew members, Erich Spehl, was regarded with suspicion by his fellow

At a May 12 hearing on the *Hindenburg* disaster, members of the U.S. Bureau of Air Commerce Investigating Board examine a diagram of the airship's mooring arrangements.

crewmen because he was known to support communist beliefs. (Communists were opposed to fascism, the political philosophy behind Hitler's regime.) Spehl himself died from severe burns, just after requesting that a cable be sent to his bride informing her that he had survived the *Hindenburg* fire. Another reason that theories of sabotage abound is that in the wreckage a Luger pistol, with one shot fired, was found.

Despite their differences of opinion, however, the theorists do all agree on one fact: that the *Hindenburg* disaster—caught on film and tape recorder, and broadcast throughout the world—convinced the world that airships were not safe for passengers . . . and wouldn't be for a very long time.

Shortly after the *Hindenburg* tragedy, the *Graf Zep-*

pelin returned to Frankfurt from Brazil and, despite having an impeccable and unmatched safety record, was removed from service. And in 1938, in the atmosphere of goodwill that was forged between Hugo Eckener and American financiers, the Helium Control Act was modified. Obviously this change would not benefit the *Hindenburg*, but the Zeppelin company did have another airship, the LZ-130, under construction at the time of the *Hindenburg* tragedy. Christened the *Graf Zeppelin II*, the new ship was designed with a number of new and possibly safer features. However, as tensions between the U.S. government and Adolf Hitler's regime increased, the promised helium never arrived. Nevertheless, the *Graf Zeppelin II* was test-flown, using hydrogen, in late 1938, and the airship continued to be tested through August 1939. Although the *Graf Zeppelin II* was believed to be the best dirigible ever built, Hitler refused to allow the ship to make a single commercial flight.

On September 1, 1939, Germany invaded Poland, and Britain declared war on the invaders; this was the start of World War II, the most costly and devastating war in history. Although Luftschiffbau Zeppelin continued to work on a "super-Zeppelin," the LZ-131, its construction was halted at the outbreak of the war. The great age of the rigid airship effectively ended. As author John Toland explains, "In March, 1940, after a bitter argument between Captain Max Pruss and Reichsmarschall Herman Göring, the original *Graf Zeppelin* and its namesake, the [former] LZ-130, were dismantled. Then two months later, the great airship hangars at Frankfurt were blown up. The day was May 6, the third anniversary of the *Hindenburg* disaster."

Other lighter-than-air craft continued to be built and flown even after the end of the great rigid dirigibles. Blimps (nonrigids) and semirigids were used during

World War II and afterward by the U.S. Navy and the Goodyear Airship Fleet. Particularly after the navy devised a method of pumping seawater into the blimps to provide ballast, and developed a new system enabling the transfer of fuel and personnel while at sea, the usefulness of lighter-than-air craft was assured.

Blimps performed a great service during World War II. The United States used them not only for routine patrols along the coast but also for missions accompanying fleets; men on these nonrigids could spot—and in at least one case destroy—German submarines (called U-boats, for Unterseeboot, literally "undersea boat"). One particularly riveting story dramatically illustrates the usefulness of navy blimps during the war:

In 1944 Lieutenant Joe Fallon was with Blimpron ZP-11, a blimp squadron that patrolled the northeastern coast of the United States, from Halifax, Nova Scotia, to New York, every other day. One trip proved particularly eventful. On August 25, off the coast of Cape Cod, Massachusetts, the crew of the 450-foot airship spotted a surfaced U-boat. Lieutenant Fallon ordered his men to drop depth charges on the German submarine.

Before the drums of explosives could be released, the U-boat fired its deck guns at the blimp. Fallon thought his airship was close enough to the submarine to sustain damage, but inexplicably, the shots missed. The depth charges, two 350-pound barrels full of TNT, did not. "Without knowing it, Lieutenant Fallon had just sunk one of Hitler's prized submarines," writes journalist Lucas Mearian.

Fallon, however, never got credit for the kill. Far from it, his commander greeted him on his return to base in South Weymouth, Massachusetts, with a terse rebuke. "Then," said Fallon, "the intelligence officers came in. One said to me, 'Joe, you stepped in a can of worms.'"

Two days later Fallon was transferred and spent the rest of the war flying blimps in South America. For 52 years Fallon never understood the reasons behind his "exile," until 1996, when he was approached by Ed Michaud, the owner of Trident Research and Recovery.

Michaud's theory, based on his own research since 1987, is that the one-of-a-kind submarine, Germany's biggest, may have been on a diplomatic mission, carrying German businessmen and consulates who wanted to negotiate a peace agreement. Other evidence supports this idea, including transcripts of German radio transmissions to the U.S. Coast Guard indicating that the submarine did not want to fire but was being attacked. If Michaud's theory is correct, it would explain why the U-boat's shots missed Fallon's blimp. Perhaps the entire story will emerge from the murky depths of history when and if Michaud is able to raise the submarine from the ocean floor, as he plans to do.

Since the navy retired its last airships in 1961, blimps have been used mostly for advertising purposes. But recently several companies have begun to reevaluate airships and examine ways in which blimps—and even rigid airships—might once again be put to practical use.

A city in the sky, the AeroCarrier is an enormous rigid airship proposed by students at the Illinois Institute of Technology. Perhaps future technological advancements will make creating a ship of its size a reality.

The Rebirth of Airships?

Charles Owen, a professor at Illinois Institute of Technology, and his design students used their imagination. Together they "imagined a city in the sky," according to writer David Ballingrud, "big enough to lift the *Queen Mary*, big enough to hold the Sears Tower—standing upright." Their airship design won a bronze prize in the 1993 International Design Competition held in Osaka, Japan. The ship—known informally as Laputa, after the floating island in Jonathan Swift's *Gulliver's Travels*— would be so huge that no hangar could contain it (1^1/$_2$ miles long, ^{3}/$_5$ mile wide, and ^{1}/$_2$ mile high). It would have to be constructed, said Owen, in a canyon. Similarly, it would be too huge to land, and so it simply wouldn't. Hovering like a giant mother ship, the Laputa would be brought supplies, fuel, and passengers by smaller, shuttle ships.

Owen did not expect to get much attention for the design, since it is impossible to build using current technology. However, according to Ballingrud, Professor Owen was surprised at the diversity of groups that approached him about the AeroCarrier project:

- The U.S. Army Corps of Engineers, looking into the feasibility of reducing barge traffic on the Mississippi River
- Iowa farmers who wanted to move grain without trains
- A Texas oil company that wanted to move extraordinarily large pieces of drilling equipment to Siberia
- A land poor developer dreaming of condominiums in the sky
- A cult leader seeking safe transport to a better place for his followers when the day of reckoning arrives

The Pentagon also sought proposals for a transport airship in 1995. Although companies such as Lockheed Martin and Federal Express responded at first, neither company pursued the idea beyond the research stage.

It seems that "Zeppelin fever" may have caught on again. In recent years several companies have been researching and developing, if not actually building, large airships. Airships hold many advantages, today's proponents insist, over airplanes and helicopters, and not just for the purpose of carrying passengers or for tourism.

The most pressing use for modern airships is cargo transport. One company with perhaps the boldest of the current projects is CargoLifter AG, based in Wiesbaden, Germany. CargoLifter plans to build a 720-foot ship capable of carrying more cargo than any aircraft—160 tons—at a speed faster than oceangoing vessels can travel. "[The CargoLifter airship] will be huge," says Mike Rentell, secretary of the United Kingdom-based Airship Association, "as long as the *Hindenburg* and twice the height."

Although CargoLifter will not be commercially profitable before 2002, the company believes that its airship will be very marketable. It will provide an inexpensive means for heavy industries that need to ship payloads like bridges and construction machinery to areas not easily reached by conventional aircraft. Companies like these are often forced to build roads and bridges to deliver their products. The CargoLifter airship can easily travel to remote areas. And because it does not need to land while delivering its cargo, no airports, hangars, or other special areas have to be built. CargoLifter has reportedly spent from $50 to $200 million in development efforts and hopes to have a prototype, the CL 160, to exhibit at the turn-of-the-century Expo 2000 in Hanover, Germany.

Reporter Kurt Loft reported on another project, known as the Cargo Airship System, or CAS, proposed by Pan Atlantic Aerospace, a company based in Ontario, Canada. "It will be like an aircraft carrier floating through the sky," notes Fred Ferguson, the company president. The purpose of CAS, of course, would be to carry enormous loads of particularly heavy or unwieldy cargo across tremendous distances and to do so at a cheaper rate than airplanes and more quickly than ships. The $50 million airship would be extremely cheap in the long run: the total amount would translate to, according to Loft, "a cost per ton of about a dime per mile."

CAS has a unique design, to say the least. Planned to be an amazing 1,500 feet long, CAS is neither blimp nor Zeppelin, but rather a kind of air train of linked but separate, helium-filled blimps. The ship's design would offer a flexibility that was markedly absent from the large rigid airships of old. According to a 1994 article, Pan Atlantic was expected to build a smaller, 600-foot version of CAS by 1995 to demonstrate its practicality and safety.

Some companies, even those that build blimps, simply

Many people today believe that airships make the most economic sense for transporting cargo loads. Here is the proto-type of one lighter-than-air transport blimp, the Flying Manta Ray. The full-scale model would haul up to 80 tons, which is four times greater than the load the largest helicopter can handle, and for a tenth of the cost.

do not believe that freight airships are economically pos-sible and are not willing to spend the great heaps of money required to develop them. But even these compa-nies recognize the advantages of airships over other modes of cargo transport. Unlike airplanes, says Loft, "airships require little constant energy to support the load; . . . create almost no noise or air pollution; need only a small service area for vertical takeoff and landing; and can travel to remote areas." When compared to freight trains and ships, airships come out ahead. Unlike trains, they have no need for rails and can travel faster than either vessel, using less fuel in the process.

But not just cargo companies are interested in a new breed of airships. In Britain, the Airship Technologies Group (ATG) has been building nonrigid blimps for years. Now the company has plans for a bigger, rigid airship, the AT-04. Their design is for a highly maneuverable, easy-to-land ship that could serve a variety of uses for the military, such as a naval minesweeper or an airborne radar platform. Commercially the airship could be used as a low-level communications satellite. Long gone are the days when safe airship landings required hundreds of ground crew members; the AT-04 would be able to land just about anywhere. It could carry up to 52 people in its gondola and travel at speeds of up to 80 miles per hour.

Airships do seem very well suited for many scientific as well as commercial uses. In Florida, scientists have used small blimps to monitor the habitats of manatees from the sky. Because airships are quieter than planes and helicopters, can hover with very little noise, and do not pollute, they are ideal for environmental work, as well as for scientific research trips to inhospitable areas.

Some companies have plans to use nonrigid blimps in new ways. Former U.S. secretary of state Alexander Haig owns a company called Sky Station, which hopes to launch blimps that would provide high-speed, high-capacity wireless broadband service, while hovering at an altitude of approximately 13 miles above the earth. High as this altitude is, it is still lower than that maintained by the telecommunications satellites currently orbiting the earth. The shorter distance between Sky Station and the earth means smaller receivers can be used and less time will be needed for transmissions. And even the projected price—more than $3 billion each—is cheaper than the

Dow Stewart, president and CEO of Rigid Airship USA, owns exclusive rights to manufacture and distribute dirigibles in the United States. His company plans to buy two 180-meter airships being built by a company in the Netherlands.

price of launching a satellite into space. Sky Stations would have the added bonus of remaining operational much longer than satellites do. The deployment of the first Sky Station is scheduled for 2000.

Some unusual uses for airships have also been suggested, such as one attributed to the Worldwide Aeros Corporation, of California. The company proposes using huge rigid airships that would hold onboard casinos.

However, the glamour purpose of the new generation of airships is undoubtedly transcontinental or transoceanic passenger service. Coopership Industries in Dallas, Texas, hopes to build a gigantic passenger airship. Dale Cooper Harris, the company's president, says the ship would carry "thousands of passengers in ultimate luxury anywhere in the world." Harris's ship would not look much like the old Zeppelins; he envisions an airship that looks like a B-2 stealth bomber but is held aloft by helium. Harris thinks that with travel speeds of up to 150 knots, the ship could easily escape bad weather and overcome strong, contrary winds.

Another excited passenger airship planner is Jonathan Hamilton, a British-born entrepreneur based in South Africa. Hamilton's company is backed by about $15 million from a variety of investors in many different nations. The company has built a small prototype of an airship in Pretoria. According to Hamilton, after the prototype has been thoroughly tested, work on its "bigger brother, *Nelson*" (named for former President Nelson Mandela) will begin. At 460 feet, the *Nelson* will carry 60 passengers in luxurious accommodations with eight-foot-high windows.

Hamilton presents a tantalizing vision of his project: "We can fly from Cape Town to London in about four days at about 500 feet so you would get to see the sights like the Alps, the Pyramids, Kilimanjaro, Victoria Falls . . . at very close range." An August 1998 article indicated a projected completion date of August 1999, but as with all the hoped-for airship projects, enormous funds are needed and are not always forthcoming.

Hamilton's critics, including Rentell of the U.K. Airship Association, are doubtful. "I don't believe for one moment that he will build an airship that will fly the Atlantic as it would have to be at least the size of the *Graf Zeppelin*, because the range of an airship is directly dependent on its size," he remarked. And the question on all potential passengers' minds since the *Hindenburg* disaster is "What about safety?"

Hamilton reassuringly claims that modern technology is up to the task. "With modern avionics and modern electrical control systems . . . you can create artificial stability through an internal navigation system. And you can keep [the airship] very stable and make it highly [maneuverable]," he declares.

It is true that materials and technology have advanced far beyond those available for the Zeppelins of the 1920 and 1930s. Instead of doped cotton cloth, for example, tear-resistant fabric can be used for the airship skin. The frame and gondola can be constructed of lightweight Kevlar and carbon materials.

Interestingly, Hamilton believes it is possible for his airships to be mass produced. Some industrial analysts believe that an airship could be built in 21 days with a labor force of 200 people if all components are available. This is a far cry from the years-long, labor-intensive construction of the *Hindenburg*.

But the company that airship enthusiasts around the world are watching is the original: Luftschiffbau Zeppelin. The company remained in business after the disappearance of rigid airships by switching its operations to machinery. In the years following World War II, the Zeppelin company repaired trucks for the French occupation forces, represented America's Caterpillar Tractor Company, and manufactured radar equipment and construction equipment.

In September 1993, the Zeppelin company founded Zeppelin Luftschifftechnik, a subsidiary with the goal to produce a prototype of a new passenger airship. The first "Zeppelin NT'" (NT stands for new technology) is the LZ N07, a 246-foot semirigid with a simple triangular framework of aluminum alloy and carbon-fiber composite. A multilayered polyester envelope surrounds helium gas cells. The LZ N07 sports computerized maneuvering, two side propellers, a tail fan, and a helicopter-type propeller that helps control pitch and yaw. Remarkably, the new ship uses the same type of propellers as the *Graf Zeppelin II*.

Incredibly, the LZ N07 weighs only 8,500 kilograms, as much as five Mercedes sedans. What's more, it requires a landing crew of only three. The LZ N07 will not be another *Graf Zeppelin*, however; it is not large enough to cross the ocean and will carry at most only twelve passengers and a crew of two.

The CEO of Zeppelin Luftschifftechnik, Klaus Hagenlocker, enthuses about the possible uses of this latest airship: "Exclusive, gentle and environment-friendly tourism is the first option, but the new Zeppelin can also carry scientific payloads, for anything from air

The Skyship 600B, housed at the NASA Ames Research Center in Moffett Field, California, stretches two-thirds the length of a football field and is as tall as a 747 jet. The $8 million blimp is the largest certified airship in operation today.

quality control to spotting oil tankers polluting coastal waters." The new Zeppelin can, unlike an airplane, fly backward and hover, which makes it quite useful for scientific flights. It will be cheaper to operate and quieter than a helicopter. Thanks to its innovative tail fan, the ship can rotate full circle while hovering in one spot.

On September 18, 1997, the LZ N07 made its first flight at Friedrichshafen, thus becoming the first commercial rigid airship to fly in more than 50 years. The flight itself was an impressive feat in light of the many skeptics who believed the project would literally never get off the ground. Most impressive of all, the Zeppelin company already has orders for five of the new ships at a cost of $7 million dollars each. The German government has ordered one to be used for scientific missions, and several companies have ordered ships to be used for advertising and tourism in Germany. But the first order to be filled was for the Skyship Cruise Company of Switzerland, which plans to begin tourist excursions over the Alps beginning in mid-2000.

Another party interested in purchasing the new Zeppelins is Christian von Wiesendonk, of Transatlantische Luftschiffahrtgesellschaft. He runs a company that is buying two airships to use for advertising and tourism. Von Wiesendonk's company would like to fly its Zeppelins to the United States to use for tours there. But first the company must wait for delivery and flight approval by U.S. authorities.

Nevertheless, Zeppelin Luftschifftechnik must first obtain a certificate of airworthiness. Because the design of the LZ N07 sought to eliminate the need for ballast, new criteria for judging airworthiness need to be created to evaluate the ship. The company is also many months behind schedule in production, and competitors are also working on latter-day airships.

As airship engineers combine the knowledge of yesterday with the technology of today, they may once again lure passengers to travel in the quiet and spacious comfort provided only by rigid airships. Long a symbol of tragedy and a lost era, the *Hindenburg* may one day be seen as a harbinger of a new golden age of safe passenger airships.

Airship Chronology

1783   Joseph-Michel and Jacques-Étienne Montgolfier send up first hot-air balloon

1852   Henri Giffard builds a self-propelled balloon

1898   Alberto Santos-Dumont flies his first airship near Paris, France

1900   Count Ferdinand von Zeppelin flies the LZ-1, his first airship, over Lake Constance, Germany

1909   Count Ferdinand von Zeppelin and associate Hugo Eckener found DELAG (Deutsche Luftschiffahrt Aktien Gesellschaft), the world's first passenger airline

1914–18   World War I: Germany uses Zeppelins to conduct air raids over England and as spy craft; Britain and United States begin building airships

1919   *June:* Per terms of the Treaty of Versailles, Allies claim Germany's Zeppelins
July: British airship R-34 becomes first aircraft to cross the Atlantic Ocean nonstop

1921   British R-38, commissioned by the U.S. Navy, crashes in the Humber River in England, killing 44 of the 49 men aboard

1922   The *Roma,* an Italian-built semirigid sold to the United States, crashes in Virginia; 33 of 44 die; becomes last American dirigible to use hydrogen gas

1923   *October:* Goodyear-Zeppelin Corporation assumes ownership of Zeppelin patents
December: The French *Dixmude,* originally the German-built L-72, disappears mysteriously over the Mediterranean Sea with 50 men aboard

1924   The USS *Shenandoah* becomes first airship to moor to a mast on a ship at sea

1925   The *Shenandoah* breaks apart near Ava, Ohio, killing 14 men

1926   General Umberto Nobile, of Italy, and Roald Amundsen, of Norway, command the *Norge* in a successful first flight to the North Pole

1928   *May:* Nobile commands the *Italia* on another polar trip; the airship crashes, killing eight; 49 days pass before the last survivor is rescued
October: First transatlantic passenger flight by an airship: the *Graf Zeppelin* carries 20 passengers and 40 crewmen

1929   The *Graf Zeppelin* completes a round-the-world tour in 21 days

Airship Chronology

1930	*July:* British airship R-100 makes first Atlantic crossing by a British airship since the R-34 crossing in 1919 *October:* British R-101 crashes near Beauvais, France; only 6 of the 54 aboard survive
1933	*April:* The USS *Akron* crashes off the coast of New Jersey, killing 73 of a crew of 76; two more die trying to rescue the *Akron* crew members Construction of the *Hindenburg* begins in Friedrichshafen, Germany
1935	The USS *Macon* crashes off the coast of California; 79 of the 81 aboard survive
1936	*March: Hindenburg*'s first flight; distributes propaganda leaflets over Germany *May: Hindenburg* begins providing regular transatlantic passenger service between Germany and the United States *October:* In famous "Millionaire's Flight," *Hindenburg* carries 73 U.S. government and industry leaders
1937	*May 6:* The *Hindenburg* bursts into flame at Lakehurst, New Jersey, killing 36 people (22 crew members, 13 passengers and one ground crew member)
1938	Goodyear Tire Company and the U.S. Navy begin building blimps that are much smaller and hardier than rigid dirigibles
1940	Goodyear-Zeppelin Corporation becomes Goodyear Aircraft; last rigid dirigible is dismantled
1939–45	World War II; blimps render excellent service during hostilities
1961	U.S. Navy decommissions remaining airships
1997	Zeppelin LZ N07 makes its first flight

Further Reading

Archbold, Rick. *Hindenburg: An Illustrated History.* New York: Warner Books, 1994.

Berliner, Don. *Aviation: Reaching for the Sky.* Minneapolis, Minn.: Oliver Press, 1997.

Day, James. *The Hindenburg Tragedy.* New York: Bookwright Press, 1989.

Dick, Harold G. *The Golden Age of the Great Passenger Airships: Graf Zeppelin and Hindenburg.* Washington, D.C.: Smithsonian Institution Press, 1985.

Perry, Phyllis J. *Ballooning.* New York: Franklin Watts, 1996.

Stacey, Thomas. *The Hindenburg* (World Disaster Series). San Diego, Calif.: Lucent Books, 1990.

Stein, R. Conrad. *The Hindenburg Disaster.* Chicago: Children's Press, 1993.

Tanaka, Shelley. *The Disaster of the Hindenburg: The Last Flight of the Greatest Airship Ever Built.* New York: Scholastic/Madison Press Books, 1993.

Toland, John. *The Great Dirigibles: Their Triumphs and Disasters.* New York: Dover Publications, 1972.

WEBSITES

"Dirigibles, Airships, Zeppelins and Blimps" (R. D. Layman)
http://www.worldwar1.com/sfzepp.htm

The Goodyear Blimp
http://www.goodyear.com/us/blimp

Herbert Morrison's recording for Chicago radio station WLS
http://www.historybuff.com/realaudio/hindenburg.html

Navy Lakehurst Historical Society
http://www.nlhs.com/

United Kingdom Airship Association
http://www.airship.demon.co.uk/

Zeppelin Luftschifftechnik GmbH home page
http://www.zeppelin-nt.com/

Index

Index

Index

GINA DE ANGELIS is a freelance writer living in southern Virginia. She holds a B.A. from Marlboro College and an M.A. from the University of Mississippi. This is her 11th book for Chelsea House.

JILL McCAFFREY has served for four years as national chairman of the Armed Forces Emergency Services of the American Red Cross. Ms. McCaffrey also serves on the board of directors for Knollwood—the Army Distaff Hall. The former Jill Ann Faulkner, a Massachusetts native, is the wife of Barry R. McCaffrey, a member of President Bill Clinton's cabinet and director of the White House Office of National Drug Control Policy. The McCaffreys are the parents of three grown children: Sean, a major in the U.S. Army; Tara, an intensive care nurse and captain in the National Guard; and Amy, a seventh grade teacher. The McCaffreys also have two grandchildren, Michael and Jack.

Picture Credits